# Working Mom's
# FAST & EASY
# KID-FRIENDLY
# MEALS

# Working Mom's
# Fast & Easy Kid-Friendly Meals

*Over 175 Yummy Recipes*
*That Will Have Your Whole Family*
*Begging for More*

## Elise M. Griffith

PRIMA PUBLISHING

**Library of Congress Cataloging-in-Publication Data**

Griffith, Elise M.
    Working mom's fast & easy kid-friendly meals : over 175 yummy recipes that will have your whole family begging for more / Elise Griffith.
        p.      cm.
    Includes index.
    ISBN 0-7615-1458-9
    1. Quick and easy cookery.  I. Title.
TX833.5.G75    1998
641.5′55—dc21                                                    98-29349
                                                                        CIP

98 99 00 01 BB 10 9 8 7 6 5 4 3 2 1

Printed in the United States of America

**How to Order**
Single copies may be ordered from Prima Publishing, P.O. Box 1260BK, Rocklin, CA 95677; telephone (916) 632-4400. Quantity discounts are also available. On your letterhead, include information concerning the in-tended use of the books and the number of books you wish to purchase.

**Visit us online at www.primapublishing.com**

This book is dedicated to my sons,
Bobby and Zachary,
who challenge me to
tickle their tastebuds every day.

# Contents

# 8 · Baking    145

## 11 · Culinary Kids  211

# Acknowledgments

This cookbook would not have been possible without my husband, Steven Griffith, whose computer expertise and nimble fingers saved the day when I lost a month's worth of work to a technological glitch. Thank you, honey, for your patience, support, encouragement, and willing palate throughout the years.

Special thanks to the many generous folks who tested recipes and cheered me on, including: Pam Branch, Luella Bouchard, Michelle Bouchard-Schmiderer, Betty Hedegus, David Morris, Leon Morris, Joyce Palm, and Audrey Parker. I appreciate each and every one of you more than you know.

Thanks to John and Lisa Meyer for farm fresh eggs throughout the development of this cookbook; they were delicious!

Finally, thanks to Susan Silva and the entire Prima staff for their dedication to providing resources for busy families everywhere.

# Introduction: Fast, Healthful Meals Are Today's Specialty

They're called "improv-moms," and they're everywhere. Chances are good that if you bought or borrowed this book, you're a whiz at improvisation. You know how to juggle the demands of family and job, multitask with the best of them, and seek out anything that makes your busy life a little easier. You enjoy some old-fashioned values and activities, but you don't have the time your mother or grandmother had available to focus on homemaking. Chances are, instead of spending hours at the ironing board, you send work clothes out to be cleaned and pressed, or you've invested in an easy-care wardrobe. Rather than spending hours in the kitchen creating everything from scratch, you're making use of a new trend in grocery stores nationwide. Welcome to the age of partially prepared foods and fast, easy "sit-down" meals!

More and more busy parents are buying meats, produce, and side-dish items that are ready to go when the dinner hour rolls around. From preroasted chickens and precooked frozen beef strips, to packaged salad greens and microwavable pastas, these convenience foods are giving restaurants a run for their money. Why? Although we're busier than ever before—an estimated 75 percent of us live in dual-income families, and the average American adult works forty-five or more hours per week—we refuse to sacrifice family meal time. It's important to us to gather our children at the table several times a week and reconnect with each other. The partially

xix

prepared foods may cost more than "from scratch" recipes, but they're still a lot less expensive than dinner for four at a traditional restaurant. By using all of the products available for today's families, we save both time and money.

One big concern is whether or not these convenience foods enhance the growing focus on healthier eating. Are we sacrificing nutrition in order to cut time in the kitchen? That depends. Federal regulations require all packaged foods to contain nutritional labeling, including the total fat, carbohydrates, and calories for each serving. By learning to read labels (if you are not already doing so), you can all make smart choices for yourself and your family. Additionally, many of the new convenience foods are available in lower-fat and fat-free varieties.

Other trends in today's kitchens include cooking only once or twice a week—which I call "marathon meal preparation"—and assembly-line foods, such as specialty pizzas, tacos, or enchiladas. More and more parents are bringing the kids into the kitchen at mealtime; virtually all of the parenting magazines include articles geared toward grooming junior chefs. It's easy to see that improv-meals help to simplify even the busiest family's life. Yet what if you have the world's pickiest eaters under your roof?

# Together in the Kitchen and at the Table

Some well-organized people plan meals a week or more in advance. They coordinate grocery store advertised specials with the menu, only buy what they need, and never, ever "wing it." However many of us are grateful to plan a meal a day or two ahead, and thrilled when it doesn't require another trip to the store. What's a busy, working mom to do? Involve the entire family.

Kids of all ages are fickle creatures. One day they love chicken, and the next day they won't touch it. Perhaps your little baseball pro begs for hot dogs, but your miniature musician demands vegetarian fare. On top of all of that, your teen discovered that his slacks either shrunk two sizes in the wash or his waistline is expanding, and he wants to trim down for an upcoming beach trip. By involving all of your children in meal planning, you can satisfy everyone's tastes (and needs) without opening up a short-order counter. Sounds impossible? What about fat-free chili dogs one night, a hearty veggie pizza the next evening, and Southwestern burgers with nachos at the end of the week? The big plus with each of these entrées is that your children can either pitch in or take over in the kitchen (depending on their ages); you merely supervise the process.

Of course, if you turned over all meal planning and preparation to the younger members of your household, you'd eat nothing but hot dogs, pizzas, and burgers for the next decade. Most kids know little—and care even less—about proper nutrition. You're concerned that they get adequate fruits, vegetables, grains, protein, calcium, iron, and other essential elements in their diet, but they're much more interested in taste. Regardless of how nutritious a meal might be, it needs to be appealing and delicious.

Many of the recipes in this book are geared not only to be simple and healthful, but to tempt the pickiest eater. Several involve more "assembly" than actual cooking, and are low fat to boot! A number of the recipes provide sneaky ways to get essential vegetables and fruits into tiny tyrants; the vegetarian section has tempting entrées that can fool the most dedicated beef eater. Do you sometimes find yourself entertaining unexpected company? You can feed a crowd with some of the recipes, and you'll still spend less than half an hour in the kitchen. Cleanup is also a snap, as all of the items are easy to prepare. Are you a dessert lover, but don't have time to bake and want to cut the fat in your favorite recipes? Then you'll want to whip up some of the no-bake, low-fat, tempting treats in chapter 8.

I believe that mealtime should be enjoyable, and even the busiest families should try to gather at the table as often as possible. No matter how hectic our schedule becomes, we try to sit down together at least five times a week for dinner. It may not always be "gourmet," but it's fast and wholesome. You really can have it all—simple, healthy, kid-pleasing meals in about twenty minutes.

# 1
# GEARING UP

Be prepared—it's a time-honored motto that, implemented in many areas of our lives, helps us achieve greater success. This doesn't mean that we'll never burn a dinner, but if the kitchen is well equipped and the pantry is stocked with basics, we'll be always be ready to rumba when mealtime rolls around. As you read through this chapter, you'll uncover ways to make time in the kitchen more enjoyable . . . and more productive.

# Gadgets and Gizmos for Busy Chefs

It used to be that a good set of pots, pans, and bakeware, a mixer, and some basic utensils were enough for an efficient kitchen. Those remain the staple items, but today's busy chef can benefit from several other useful, time-saving tools. Is it worth the investment? I think so. You can save over 100 hours per year in the kitchen with some of the gadgets and gizmos available on the market today. The price tag of new equipment is dropping as more and more cooks across the country look for ways to carve more time for fun and family. And if you're fortunate enough to have a resale shop nearby, you may be able to buy them for less than half their original price.

## Pots and Pans

- Look for durable nonstick pots and pans that are both sturdy and heavy. Although most families don't require professional quality equipment, the lowest price point isn't necessarily the best value. Thin aluminum pans with a light Teflon coating will become warped and scratched inside of a year. If you plan to spend a lot of time in the kitchen cooking gourmet meals, and you have about $500 lying around, you can get top-of-the-line cookware that will last a lifetime. Fortunately, a set of new, good-quality cookware should only cost about $100. Farberware, Regal "Club," and T-Fal are brands that have all earned high ratings with reviewers and professional cooks. Purchase pieces one at a time if the cost of a full set doesn't fit your budget.
- Useful pots and pans include: 1-quart, 2-quart, and 5-quart pots with lids; 8-inch and 10- or 11-inch frying pans; and nonstick square griddles—ideal for weekend breakfasts and grilled cheese sandwiches.
- Nonstick bakeware is also essential for healthy, low-fat cooking. An added bonus is that clean-up is easier. You'll

need one or two cookie sheets, round and rectangular cake pans, and a twelve-cup muffin pan. You might also wish to purchase two loaf pans, a square cake pan, and a pizza pan. Chicago Metallic, Ekco, and Revere Ware offer affordable, durable, nonstick sets and individual pieces. Prices range from $5 to $15 per piece, or $20 to $60 per set.

## Plug-Ins

- The aroma of freshly baked bread is almost universally comforting. Yet how many busy, working moms have the time to mix, knead, wait for the dough to rise, knead again, shape, wait for a second rise, and then bake for almost an hour? Perhaps a few times a year we'll pull out our favorite recipes, call the kids into the kitchen, and prepare home-made loaves. With a bread machine, your family can enjoy fresh bread any time. For an investment of about $50 to $75 (new) or $25 to $40 (used), you can get a durable, low-noise, basic model that's capable of baking regular and large-sized white, wheat, and sweet breads. For $20 to $30 more, you can get a machine that has dessert options. If you prefer traditional-looking loaves, expect to pay in the neighborhood of $100 for a new machine, or $70 for a quality used machine through a reseller. Brands that have done well in consumer tests include Black and Decker, Oster, Toastmaster, and West Bend.
- No busy kitchen would be complete without a slow cooker, such as a Crock-Pot. If you never thought slow cooking could produce fast healthy meals, you'll want to try a few of the recipes in chapter 5. When shopping for a slow cooker to meet your needs, look for brands and models that offer removable stoneware crocks that can be safely washed in your dishwasher. Prices range from $25 to $40, depending on size and brand. In consumer tests, Proctor Silex, Rival, and West Bend models earned the highest marks.

- Do you remember the harvest gold and avocado electric stand mixers of the 1970s? Chances are, there was one nestled under the cabinet in the kitchen of your childhood home. Today's electric mixers have come a long way, but basic models still whip up tasty batters. If you do a lot of baking from scratch, a stand mixer is a good investment. However, if you're more inclined to pull a packaged mix from the pantry, and your counter space is limited, you'll find a hand-mixer more useful. Unfortunately, hand-mixers have an outdated reputation for being much less powerful than their larger, pricier relatives. Farberware sells a very powerful, five-speed model that includes regular beaters, wire beaters, and dough hooks for about $35. Other models that can take a lot of beating include Black and Decker, Braun, and KitchenAid. Expect to pay a modest $20 to $40 for any 200-watt model.

- For fast preparation of fresh produce, along with other useful tasks, a food processor saves today's busy cook hours of time. If you already own one, you know that you can chop, dice, shred, slice, juice, blend, and mix a multitude of ingredients with this relatively small appliance. Sizes range from 1½-cup-capacity choppers to 11-cup professional models, and prices range from $20 to $200 (or more) for new machines. When you're feeding a family of four or five, a basic 6-cup model with slicing, shredding, and chopping attachments should be adequate, and will cost about $50. For gourmet cooks who prepare many meals and treats from scratch, an investment of $130 will buy a multifunction processor that also includes a dough hook, cream attachment, and citrus juicer. Durable, affordable brands include Black and Decker, Braun, Cuisinart, and KitchenAid.

- Many homes and apartments now come fully equipped with a built-in microwave oven. If you've been using one for a while, try to imagine cooking for one day without it. Today's families use microwave ovens for everything from warming coffee and leftovers to popping popcorn and roasting meat. These time-saving appliances seem "priceless" for the busy cook. You can expect to pay anywhere from $100 to $200 for a basic 1-cubic-foot-capacity model or larger (a larger model can accommodate full meals for a family of four). It's worth the investment. Look for a microwave oven that includes multiple power settings, a defrost option, one-touch keys for common tasks, and a child lock. Most experts recommend 1,000 watts of power; and many new models have shower-wave or double-emission wave systems that are believed to be safer than earlier microwave ovens. Sanyo, Sharp, and Whirlpool are all reputable brands with good consumer reviews.

• A steamer/rice cooker is also a wonderful, inexpensive appliance that affords healthier cooking and eating. Steamed fresh vegetables retain all of their original nutrients, and are ready in minutes with one of these gadgets. Cooks can also expect perfect rice (white, brown, or long grain) every time when using a steamer/rice cooker. What you may not have known is that you can also cook low-fat meats, dumplings, and other foods using your electric steamer. Black and Decker, Farberware, Salton, and Sunbeam earn the highest ratings with nutritionists and busy cooks. Model sizes range from 8-cup to 8-quart capacities, and sell for between $25 and $55.

Those are the basic appliances for today's well-equipped kitchen. Depending on your needs, tastes, time, available space, and interests, you might also consider an electric rotisserie, electric ice cream freezer, clay baker, food grinder, pasta maker, toaster oven, waffle iron, or any of the other dozens of gizmos available on the market. Some cooks can't live without a heavy-duty blender. Others insist that fondue pots will never go out of style. It seemed like every newly married couple in the 1980s received an electric wok as a gift, and not all of them were unloaded through garage sales. Choose the appliances that will do the most work for you, and don't forget to scour resale shops for bargain prices.

# Stocking Up on Basic Ingredients

A well-stocked pantry is every working parent's dream, yet many of us dash in and out of the grocery store several times a week for a bag full of items because larger shopping trips are difficult to squeeze into a busy schedule. Avoid long lines at the checkout by planning early-morning grocery trips on the weekends, or pop in after 10 P.M. on week nights. The following grocery list includes all of the basics for fast, family meals:

## Nonperishable Items

- cooking spray
- light canola or olive oil
- fat-free mayonnaise and salad dressings
- individual serving cups of applesauce (these are ½-cup servings, perfect for baking)
- sweet potatoes (or 4-ounce jars of strained sweet potato baby food)
- corn flakes
- bread crumbs
- instant mashed potatoes
- instant rice
- thin spaghetti
- vegetable pastas
- quick-cooking oats
- reduced-fat granola-type cereals
- marshmallows
- canned kidney, pinto, white, and black beans
- canned diced tomatoes

- canned vegetable broth and reduced-fat creamed soups
- granulated, powdered, and brown sugars
- whole wheat flour
- all-purpose flour
- packaged biscuit mix
- packaged corn muffin mix
- Rapid Rise (or bread machine) yeast
- baking powder
- cornstarch
- fat-free instant pudding
- powdered milk (premeasured envelopes are the most convenient)
- spices and seasonings
- frozen vegetables and vegetable/pasta mixtures
- frozen apple and orange juice

## From the Dairy Section

- nonfat sour cream
- nonfat yogurt (plain and flavored)
- nonfat cream cheese
- fresh eggs (and/or egg substitute)
- 2%-fat milk
- reduced-fat shredded cheeses
- refrigerated canned dough (biscuits, crescent rolls, pizza dough, and so on)
- reduced-fat margarine

## Fresh and Frozen Meats

- extra-lean cuts of beef
- extra-lean cuts of pork
- boneless, skinless chicken breasts (or thighs)
- ground turkey
- fresh or frozen seafood

- frozen (cooked) diced chicken or beef
- frozen meatballs

## Produce

- packaged salad greens
- packaged sliced mushrooms
- onions
- green and red peppers
- assorted fruits (in season)
- assorted vegetables (in season)

## Time-Saving Items

- frozen diced green peppers
- frozen diced onions
- minced garlic in a jar
- roasted red peppers in a jar
- dried herbs
- precooked, roasted whole chicken (from the deli section)
- thick-sliced deli meats (cut into strips for recipes)
- boil-in-bag pastas and rice
- reduced-fat or fat-free salad dressings (for marinades and sauces)
- reduced-fat or fat-free frozen whipped topping
- prepared pizza crusts (such as Boboli brand)
- prepared graham cracker pie shells
- heavy-duty aluminum foil
- freezer bags
- disposable foil pans

# Shelf Life and Storage Tips

Can't remember what's in that plastic container in the back of the freezer? Or how long it's been nestled there? Do you have boxes of dry goods that have sat in the cupboard for months? Television news reports warn us about the dangers of tainted foods, but how many of us really know how "safe" our food is? One way you can be sure the foods you're eating are untainted is to store them properly and keep track of expiration dates.

## Dry Goods and Canned Foods

- Virtually all packaged foods have an expiration date printed or stamped on the label or box. This date is the last day the store can sell the items; packages that are approaching the expiration are often sold at reduced prices. If you'd like to take advantage of the sale prices, you'll need to use the foods immediately or freeze, if possible.
- Cake mixes, flour, cereals, and other dry goods can be stored in a cool, dry pantry or cupboard for several months. As the expiration date approaches, the same items can be stored in airtight containers in the freezer for up to three months. Be sure to label the freezer bags or containers carefully, noting on the label the date you placed them in the freezer. Items containing yeast (such as packaged bread mixes) should not be frozen in their dry state; it's better to prepare the dough, allow it to rise, punch it down, shape, and then freeze, ready to bake.
- If you live in a warm or humid area, store even your freshest dry goods in airtight containers in the pantry or cupboard. This prevents bacterial and insect contamination, as well as the growth of molds. Be sure your containers are clean and dry before placing any food in them, and seal them tightly. For the safest possible storage, attach labels on the containers, noting the expiration dates from the original packaging. Place an open box of baking soda in the pantry or cupboard as well. Not only will the baking soda

absorb odors, it will help to absorb some of the moisture from the air.

- Canned foods have a long shelf life—as long as the can is not dented, swollen, or showing signs of rust. Again, it's important to check the label dates. You can drain and freeze some canned goods if the expiration date is approaching and you know you won't have the chance to use them quickly. Keep in mind that tomatoes and beans do not freeze well (once thawed, they turn to mush).

## Frozen Meats

- Careful handling and thawing of meat is essential, as even the tiniest bit of bacteria causes serious illness in small children. When you've brought the groceries in, wash your hands thoroughly with soap and water before opening, handling, and freezing meats of any kind.
- Label freezer bags carefully, and use the frozen meats within a month or two. Although some meats are considered "safely frozen" beyond the two-month mark, they'll have less chance of contamination (and will taste better) when used quickly.
- Always thaw frozen meats slowly in the refrigerator or quickly in a microwave oven, rather than on a countertop.

## Frozen Fruits and Vegetables

- Frozen vegetables and fruits have a long freezer life. Unopened packages can keep safely for six months or more in a storage freezer, or up to six months in the freezer section of your refrigerator.
- Freezer burn can be a problem if the temperature in your freezer is above 32 degrees, or if you live in a humid area. There's nothing worse than planning dinner and discovering that the vegetables are inedible.

- Once opened, reseal freezer packages tightly and use the items as soon as possible.

## Perishable Foods

- We've all dealt with soggy lettuce and sprouted potatoes. I sometimes refer to the "vegetable crisper" as the "vegetable rotter." One reason refrigerated produce items become too ripe or moldy is that the drawer contains fungus spores. Be sure to clean out the drawer at least once a month with an antibacterial cleanser or lemon juice. Set the humidity gauge at "low" if your refrigerator has one. Keep a fresh box of opened baking soda on a refrigerator shelf, and a few tablespoons of baking soda in small, open containers in the drawers to reduce odors and humidity.
- Have you ever noticed that fruit baskets containing bananas tend to ripen very quickly? Bananas produce a gas that ripens surrounding fruit at an accelerated pace. So unless you plan to eat all of the fruit quickly, store your bananas in a separate area (away from other produce).
- Apples, peaches, pears, nectarines, and other fresh fruits will keep on the counter for a week, and in the refrigerator for two weeks or more with care.
- Keep potatoes and other root vegetables in dark, cool, dry storage (not in the refrigerator). Most varieties of potatoes will remain fresh for two weeks or more if kept away from light and humidity. Before cooking, remove any green patches or sprouts.
- Consume dairy products such as milk, eggs, and yogurt as soon as possible after purchase. Many cheeses can be stored in the refrigerator for a few weeks safely; remove and discard any mold from hard cheeses before storing or serving. Once opened, use packaged shredded cheese within a week or two for safety. If you buy farm-fresh eggs that have not been treated with chemicals or antibiotics,

use them within one week of purchase and cook them thoroughly.

- Baked goods can be stored in airtight packages in the freezer for several weeks or months. This includes breads, cakes, biscuits, cookies, and other products. The colder your freezer, the longer they'll remain fresh. Label items with the date that they were placed in the freezer, and thaw them in the refrigerator for best results.

## Tips for Special Diets

- If allergies are a problem in your family, you might find that the suggested list of pantry and refrigerator items won't work for you. Many people today are on a restricted diet of some kind, which can complicate mealtime for a busy parent. Fortunately, there are wonderful products on the market for just about every dietary problem or concern.
- People with diabetes and ADD require low-sugar diets. Try substituting granulated Equal Measure (a sugar substitute) for the granulated sugar in favorite recipes. Other alternatives include frozen fruit juice concentrates (thawed), or pureed fruits and sweet vegetables. Purchase sugar-free puddings, gelatin, cereals, and other products that have been developed for sugar-restricted menus. Read labels carefully; many canned foods and other packaged items contain sugars. Ground cinnamon, ginger, and nutmeg add sweetness to homemade cookies, muffins, and cakes— without the sugar.
- Low-sodium diets can also restrict food choices. Did you know that the average can of condensed soup has a day's worth of sodium in each serving? Or that the sodium content of many packaged mixes is considered too high for most heart patients? Even reduced-sodium products can contain too much salt for severely restricted diets. Try sodium-free chips, crackers, snacks, and canned foods.

12 Gearing Up

Frozen vegetables without seasonings or sauces are also good choices. Rely on herbs, onions, garlic, diced green peppers, and lemon juice to season meats, poultry, and seafood.

- Children and adults with lactose intolerance might be surprised to discover milk and milk by-products in cold cuts, but it's true: Many varieties of salami contain milk, whey, or sodium casienate (milk protein). Margarine is another hidden source of dairy; buy 100 percent vegetable oil varieties. Canned spaghetti sauce often contains milk products, as do many brands of crackers, snacks, and breads. Careful label reading can help you avoid the hidden milk in many processed foods. Many soy-based substitutes are available in the dairy section of your grocery store. If soy is also a problem in your home, consider goat milk and cheeses for cooking and baking. Many farmers have refined the diet of their animals so that the goat milk tastes nearly the same as cow's milk, but the proteins and sugars in goat milk are often more easily digested (reducing the chance of discomfort or allergic reaction).

# Preparing Recipes vs. Assembling Meals

When it comes to meal preparation, many of us are not following grandma's all-day-in-the-kitchen example. That's good news for today's food industry, and it's better news for busy parents everywhere. We've never had more choices when it comes to shopping for quick and easy-to-prepare foods.

The fastest-growing sections in grocery stores today cater to meal assembly. We want "home-cooked" quality without the fuss, and it's available—at a price. A deli-roasted chicken, for example, sells at a 50 percent higher price than an uncooked chicken of comparable size. If time is money, however, then it may be worth the extra expense to dash in and out of the grocery store with dinner in the bag. In less than ten minutes, you can grab everything you need for a delicious, satisfying meal that you'll have on the table before the kids start to bicker. Tonight's menu might look like this:

grilled beef ribs from the deli
foil-wrapped baked potatoes from the deli
fresh, hot rolls from the bakery
packaged salad greens
diced and packaged assorted fresh vegetables
frozen yogurt pops

You'll probably spend between $15 and $17 for the meal; but depending on the size of your family, that will include your brown bag lunch for tomorrow and a snack or two. It's called improvisational cooking, and it usually includes nothing more than quickly warming the food in your oven before serving. According to the food industry and national marketing gurus, this is how we'll be cooking in the twenty-first century.

If you enjoy getting your hands dirty in the kitchen like I do, the recipes in this book are for you. Instead of shopping for ready-to-go meals, you can shop for items that require some cooking time but with less hassle than from-scratch recipes. If you take a quick stroll past the refrigerated butcher section in your local supermarket, you'll discover marinated uncooked meats, assembled uncooked meatballs, cellophane-wrapped packages of roast and vegetables, breaded pork chops, diced and formed potato products, and more. You can find seasoned, uncooked strips of chicken, beef, or pork, and fresh sausages. In the frozen food aisle, you'll find frozen mashed potatoes that can be ready in minutes, and sliced garlic bread that just needs heating.

Even cooking from scratch has taken on a new meaning with faster, easier recipes. If it takes more than an hour or requires more than a dozen ingredients, we probably won't try it. We love the taste of food prepared with love, we just want to accomplish our goal quickly and simply. Sometimes we tackle more elaborate meals, and sometimes we go all out, but most of our recipes have been pared down and streamlined. When our budgets or diets don't allow for prepared and partially prepared foods, cooking from scratch is essential. Did you know that you can prepare two or three days' worth of meals during one session in the kitchen?

Whether you buy a precooked dinner or prepare it from scratch, you can set and maintain a goal of sitting down together for a family meal at least five times a week. If you have picky eaters in your home, don't worry. Here are some menu suggestions based on all three options of meal-making (you'll find the recipes in this book):

**Sunday:** Specially Seasoned Sirloin and Vegetables, Hearty Oat Bread, tossed salad, and Fast and Low-Fat Pumpkin Pie

**Monday:** Last-Minute Beef Stew over rice, tossed salad, and Chewy Oatmeal Bars (also great for school lunches)

**Tuesday:** Chili con Corny, warm flour tortillas, and Rainbow Melon Wedges

**Wednesday:** Last-Minute Beefy Barbecue Wraps (using leftover chili and tortillas), Creamy Coleslaw, and Frozen Yogurt Pops

**Thursday:** Deli-roasted chicken (purchased), pasta salad (purchased), Simple Spinach and Broccoli, rolls (purchased), and Easiest Boston Cream Pie

**Friday:** Elementary Fajita Pitas (using leftover chicken), tossed salad, and Fruit and Easy Mousse

**Saturday:** Spaghetti and Spicy Meatballs, Easy Italian Pasta Salad, garlic bread, and Almost-Homemade Apple Pie

This cookbook contains ideas to help you make the most of your grocery store, household budget, and time in the kitchen. All of the recipes are quick, easy, and kid-tested for appeal. Since many of the recipes involve assembly, your children can pitch in with the preparation. Who knows? Mealtime might become the most relaxing part of everyone's day . . . the way it used to be.

# 2
# BREAKFASTS

Cranberry-Orange Bars
Out-the-Door Breakfast
Citrus Breakfast Shake
Breakfast Plum-Style "Pudding"
Make-Ahead Carrot-Bran Muffins
Breakfast Brown Rice Pudding
Best Breakfast Turnovers
Sweet Potato Pancakes
All-in-One Cheese Omelet
Bed and Breakfast Quiche
Easy, Cheesy Breakfast Cobbler
Morning Sunrise Cornbread

Breakfast is often the most overlooked (and rushed) meal of the day. It's so simple to grab a processed cereal bar as we dash out the door, or pour a quick bowl of sugar-sweetened puffs before the children's bus arrives. For many years we've been reading that eating a good breakfast helps us perform at our best, but few of us feel we have the necessary time to begin each day with a balanced, healthy meal.

This chapter provides recipes for make-ahead breakfast treats that are portable and healthy. If you have a little more time, there are recipes for quick, easy alternatives to family favorites. Would you like to prepare a special family meal on a weekend morning? You'll find recipes for those, too. And when friends or relatives are visiting, you'll want to try some of the fit-for-a-crowd recipes that are worthy of your own "Bed and Breakfast" kitchen.

Here's a hint—involve your children in the preparation, and you may find that morning rush hour is a lot less stressful.

# Cranberry-Orange Bars

*These fast, fruity bars are ideal for days when it's your turn to taxi the carpool gang, or when you hit the snooze button one too many times.*

Estimated preparation time: 10 minutes
Makes 12 generous bars

1. Place margarine, marmalade, and marshmallows in a large glass mixing bowl.
2. Microwave on high for 2 minutes. Stir. If marshmallows are not completely melted, microwave on high for 1 additional minute.
3. Stir in cereal until well combined and completely coated with marshmallow creme.
4. Lightly coat a $9 \times 13$-inch baking dish with cooking oil spray. Spread cereal mixture evenly over the bottom. Using a sheet of waxed paper or plastic wrap, gently press cereal mixture tightly and evenly into the pan. Refrigerate until ready to serve.

2 tablespoons reduced-fat margarine
2 tablespoons orange marmalade
3 cups miniature marshmallows
1 box (13 ounces) cranberry almond crunch cereal
cooking oil spray

# Out-the-Door Breakfast

1 small banana
¾ cup skim milk
1 container (8 ounces) nonfat
    vanilla yogurt
¼ cup orange juice
2 tablespoons wheat germ

*Why spend the money for canned breakfast drinks when this delicious, fruity "shake" is ready in minutes?*

Estimated preparation time: 5 minutes
Makes about 2 cups

**1.** Place all ingredients in blender and pulse until smooth.

# Citrus Breakfast Shake

*If your children love those frothy orange drinks at the mall, they'll love to start the day with this fruit smoothie!*

1 cup drained canned
    mandarin oranges
¾ cup skim milk
1 container (8 ounces) nonfat
    lemon yogurt
¼ cup orange juice
2 tablespoons wheat germ

Estimated preparation time: 5 minutes
Makes about 2 cups

**1.** Place all ingredients in blender and pulse until smooth.

# Breakfast Plum-Style "Pudding"

1 package (0.3 ounces) sugar-free cherry gelatin
3 cups low-fat granola with raisins
1 teaspoon cinnamon
1 teaspoon nutmeg

*Dessert for breakfast? Your children will think that's what they're eating when they try this rich, creamy "pudding."*

Estimated preparation time: 8 minutes
Estimated refrigerated time: overnight
Makes 8 servings

1. Mix gelatin as directed on box and pour into sealable storage bowl. Add remaining ingredients and refrigerate overnight.
2. Spoon into small bowls or mugs for a quick, tasty breakfast or snack.

# Make-Ahead Carrot-Bran Muffins

*These "bakery-style" muffins provide a healthy, hearty, and portable breakfast, and they also make a delicious snack!*

Estimated preparation time: 15 minutes
Estimated baking time: 15 minutes
Makes 2 dozen bakery-style muffins

1. Preheat oven to 375 degrees.
2. Place bran cereal in a small bowl, pour in boiling water, and let stand until softened.
3. Combine carrot bread mix, baking soda, egg substitute, and milk in a large bowl, then add softened bran mix and stir until blended. Fold raisins and pecans into batter until just moistened.
4. Line nonstick muffin tins with a light coating of cooking oil spray or cupcake papers. Pour in batter.
5. Bake for 15 minutes, or until muffins spring back when lightly touched.

2 cups bran cereal
2 cups boiling water
1 package (5 or 6 ounces) carrot quick-bread mix
2 teaspoons baking soda
2 containers (4 ounces each) egg substitute, thawed
2 cups skim milk
1 cup raisins
½ cup chopped pecans
cooking oil spray (optional)

# Breakfast Brown Rice Pudding

2 cups cooked brown rice
1 cup nonfat milk
2 teaspoons sugar
$\frac{1}{3}$ cup raisins
1 container (4 ounces) egg
    substitute, thawed
$\frac{1}{4}$ teaspoon ground cinnamon

*On cold, wintry mornings, this breakfast pudding is sure to be a hit—and it's nutritious!*

Estimated preparation time: 2 minutes
Estimated cooking time: 17 minutes, including time to set
Makes 4 servings

1. Place rice, milk, and sugar in a medium nonstick pot. Cook over medium-low heat for 10 minutes, stirring occasionally.
2. Add raisins and cook for an additional 2 minutes, then remove from heat.
3. Slowly stir in egg substitute, sprinkle with cinnamon, cover, and let sit for 5 minutes.

# Best Breakfast Turnovers

*To cut down on preparation time in the morning, prepare the dried fruits for these turnovers ahead of time and store them in a zip-top bag until ready to use.*

½ cup dried apricots, chopped
½ cup dried apples, chopped
½ cup raisins
¼ cup shredded coconut
    (optional)
2 tablespoons orange juice
2 cans (8 ounces each)
    refrigerated reduced-
    fat crescent rolls
cooking oil spray
2 or 3 tablespoons nonfat milk
    (optional)

Estimated preparation time: 5 minutes
Estimated baking time: 12 minutes
Makes 8 turnovers

1. Preheat oven to 375 degrees.
2. Combine fruit, coconut, and juice in small mixing bowl.
3. Unroll sheets of crescent roll dough and separate into 16 individual triangles.
4. Place 1 or 2 tablespoons of the fruit mixture in the middle of 8 of the triangles. Carefully arrange each of the remaining triangles on top of the fruited ones. Using a fork, press all edges together tightly.
5. Lightly coat a cookie sheet with cooking oil spray. Place the turnovers on the cookie sheet and brush tops of turnovers with nonfat milk if desired. Bake for about 12 minutes, or until golden brown.

# Sweet Potato Pancakes

1 can (16 ounces) sweet
    potatoes, drained
1 egg
$\frac{2}{3}$ cup nonfat milk
1 cup flour
$\frac{1}{2}$ teaspoon salt
1 teaspoon baking powder

*What could be better than pancakes on a weekend morning? These are sweet, nutritious, low in fat, and sure to please your gang.*

Estimated preparation time: 5 minutes
Estimated cooking time: 4 to 6 minutes each
Makes 8 4-inch pancakes

1. Preheat nonstick griddle or skillet over medium heat.
2. Place sweet potatoes, egg, and milk in blender and puree. Add flour, salt, and baking powder and whip until creamy-smooth.
3. Pour batter onto hot griddle to make 4-inch circles. Cook 2 to 3 minutes on each side, turning carefully. Serve with a light syrup or powdered sugar and cinnamon.

# All-in-One Cheese Omelet

*Even if you've never made an omelet, you'll get raves for this easy recipe.*

Estimated preparation time: 5 minutes
Estimated cooking time: 5 to 7 minutes
Makes 4 servings

1. Preheat medium nonstick skillet over medium-low heat.
2. Place eggs, cottage cheese, and milk in blender and pulse until well blended.
3. Lightly spray hot skillet with cooking oil spray and immediately add egg mixture. Reduce heat to low, sprinkle on pepper and shredded cheese, cover, and cook for 5 minutes.
4. Remove to plate or platter, slice, and serve.

4 eggs, or 2 containers (4 ounces each) egg substitute, thawed
1 cup low-fat cottage cheese
½ cup nonfat milk
cooking oil spray
¼ teaspoon coarsely ground pepper
⅓ cup reduced-fat shredded cheddar cheese

# Bed and Breakfast Quiche

2 cartons (4 ounces each) egg
        substitute, thawed
¾ cup nonfat sour cream
1 cup shredded fat-free
        cheddar cheese
2 green onions, finely diced
½ cup leftover chopped
        broccoli, or fresh,
        steamed broccoli that
        has cooled
¼ cup reduced-fat imitation
        bacon bits (optional)
1 purchased prepared frozen
        pie shell, thawed

*Your family and guests will feel special when you serve this delicious, low-fat quiche.*

Estimated preparation time: 5 minutes
Estimated baking time: 25 minutes, including time to set
Makes 8 servings

1. Preheat oven to 400 degrees.
2. Place egg substitute, sour cream, and shredded cheese in blender; pulse until smooth and well combined. Add onions, broccoli, and imitation bacon bits. Pulse twice to chop—be careful not to pulverize the vegetables.
3. Pour egg mixture into thawed, uncooked pie shell. Cover pie crust edges with thin strips of aluminum foil to protect them from burning.
4. Bake for approximately 20 minutes, or until the top of quiche is golden brown.
5. Remove from oven and allow to cool for 5 minutes before slicing and serving. Quiche should be soft-firm when cut.

# Easy, Cheesy Breakfast Cobbler

*Try this recipe when you're celebrating a special event or holiday with your family and friends—it makes a wonderful addition to an informal brunch menu.*

Estimated preparation time: 5 minutes
Estimated baking time: 15 minutes
Makes 8 to 10 servings

1. Preheat oven to 375 degrees.
2. Lightly coat a $9 \times 13$-inch baking pan with cooking oil spray.
3. Arrange biscuits in bottom of baking dish.
4. Place fruit on top of biscuits, and sprinkle with cornstarch. Sprinkle shredded cheese over fruit.
5. Bake for 15 minutes, or until biscuits have puffed and cheese has melted.

cooking oil spray
1 can (5 ounces) refrigerated reduced-fat biscuits
2 cups fresh, frozen, or canned peaches, diced
1 cup fresh or frozen berries (blueberries or raspberries work best)
1 tablespoon cornstarch
1 cup shredded fat-free cheddar cheese

# Morning Sunrise Cornbread

1 package (7.5 ounces) corn
    muffin mix
1 can (15 ounces) cream-style
    corn
½ cup low-fat cottage cheese
¼ cup water
cooking oil spray
fresh berries or fruit for
    garnish (optional)

*This cornbread is an all-day favorite in my home— for breakfast, dinner, or dessert.*

Estimated preparation time: 5 minutes
Estimated baking time: 15 to 17 minutes
Makes 6 servings

1. Preheat oven to 400 degrees.
2. Place corn muffin mix, corn, cottage cheese, and water in a medium bowl and stir until well combined. Batter will be lumpy.
3. Lightly coat a $9 \times 9$-inch baking dish with cooking oil spray and pour in batter.
4. Bake for 15 to 17 minutes or until a toothpick inserted in the center comes out clean.
5. Remove from oven and allow to cool slightly. Serve warm with fresh berries or fruit garnish, if desired.

# 3
# LUNCH-BOX
# WINNERS

Freezer Meat-and-Cheese Rolls
Freezer Creamy Vegetable Rolls
Freezer Hero Sandwich Rolls
Hearty Thermos Meaty Stew
Savory Thermos Rice Medley
Toddler-Sized Meaty Biscuit Bites
Preschool Peanut Butter-and-Fruity Roll-Ups
Elementary Fajita Pitas
Easy Cheese Pizza Sandwiches
Triple-Decker Turkey Sandwich
"Oh Bologna" Sandwiches
Turkey-Berry Sandwich Treats
Chicken Confetti Pitas
Cool, Creamy Ham and Fettuccini Salad
Happy Burgers and Fries
Nothing But Nachos

On busy mornings, it can be nearly impossible to get everyone dressed, fed, and out of the door on time; preparing lunches for everyone only adds to the frenzy. That's why food manufacturers came up with packaged lunches that can be slipped into a lunch pail. But those items aren't necessarily healthy or nutritious. Although school lunches are more affordable than restaurant or fast-food meals, my budget can't accommodate hot lunches every day . . . or can it?

This chapter will cover make-ahead recipes using leftovers and staple pantry items to ease morning rush-hour stress. For the sandwich lovers in your home, you'll find recipes listed according to age and taste—including recipes for budding connoisseurs. You don't have to give up fast-food lunches, and you don't have to pay fast-food prices; there are also recipes for healthy alternatives to family favorites. Each of the recipes listed in this chapter have been developed to take the worry out of feeding your lunch crew quickly, nutritiously, and affordably!

# Freezer Meat-and-Cheese Rolls

*Your children will love to help you assemble these delicious sandwiches, and it's a good way to use up leftover dinner meats.*

1 pound frozen bread dough, thawed
2 cups diced cooked ham, chicken, turkey, or beef
1 cup reduced-fat shredded cheddar cheese

Estimated preparation time: 10 minutes
Estimated baking time: 15 to 20 minutes
Makes: 4 servings

1. Divide bread dough into 4 equal portions, and roll each portion into an 8-inch circle.
2. Place ½ cup diced meat and ¼ cup shredded cheese in the center of each dough circle. Fold tightly burrito-style, and place seam-side down on a nonstick cookie sheet.
3. Slide the cookie sheet onto the center rack of a cold oven and set the temperature to 375 degrees. Bake for 15 to 20 minutes, or until golden brown.
4. Remove from oven and allow to cool.
5. Place rolls in sandwich-sized freezer bags and freeze for up to 3 weeks. Place individual rolls in lunch boxes in the morning, and they will thaw by lunchtime.

Note: For "power baking," prepare this plus the following two recipes (at the same time), and you'll have plenty of last-minute sandwiches.

# Freezer Creamy Vegetable Rolls

1 pound frozen bread dough,
    thawed
4 tablespoons garden
    vegetable-style cream
    cheese spread
2 cups packaged broccoli slaw

*If you think vegetarian sandwiches are less hearty than those with meat, these will surprise you!*

Estimated preparation time: 10 minutes
Estimated baking time: 15 to 20 minutes
Makes 4 servings

1. Divide bread dough into 4 equal portions. Roll each portion into an 8-inch circle.
2. Spread 1 tablespoon cream cheese in the center of each dough circle; spoon ½ cup shredded vegetables on top of cream cheese. Fold tightly burrito-style and place seam-side down on nonstick cookie sheet.
3. Slide the cookie sheet onto the center rack of a cold oven and set the temperature to 375 degrees. Bake for 15 to 20 minutes, or until golden brown.
4. Remove from oven and allow to cool.
5. Place in sandwich-sized freezer bags and freeze for up to 3 weeks. Place individual rolls in lunch boxes in the morning, and they will thaw by lunchtime.

# Freezer Hero Sandwich Rolls

*My guys love Italian-style foods, and these sandwiches are lunchbox favorites—add fresh fruit or salad, and your gang will enjoy a delicious, balanced meal.*

1 pound frozen bread dough, thawed
4 teaspoons fat-free Italian dressing
4 slices turkey or beef salami
2 1-ounce slices reduced-fat cheese (any kind), cut in half

Estimated preparation time: 10 minutes
Estimated baking time: 15 to 20 minutes
Makes 4 servings

1. Divide bread dough into 4 equal portions and roll each portion into an 8-inch circle.
2. Spread 1 teaspoon Italian dressing in the center of each dough circle. Top with 1 slice salami and ½ slice cheese. Fold tightly burrito-style and place seam-side down on a nonstick cookie sheet.
3. Slide the cookie sheet onto the center rack of a cold oven and set the temperature to 375 degrees. Bake for 15 to 20 minutes, or until golden brown.
4. Remove from oven and allow to cool.
5. Place in sandwich-sized freezer bags and freeze for up to 3 weeks. Place individual rolls in lunch boxes in the morning, and they will thaw by lunchtime.

# Hearty Thermos Meaty Stew

1 cup prepared mashed
    potatoes
⅓ cup water
1 teaspoon beef or chicken
    bouillon (depending on
    meat used)
¼ teaspoon coarsely ground
    pepper
2 cups diced cooked chicken,
    turkey, pork, or beef
2 cups cooked vegetables
    (leftovers work well)

*This lunchtime entrée can warm up even the coldest day, and it's lower in fat than canned stew.*

Estimated preparation time: 7 minutes
Estimated cooking time: 13 minutes, including reheating
Makes 4 servings

1. Place mashed potatoes, water, bouillon, and pepper in a medium nonstick pot.
2. Cook uncovered over medium-low heat, stirring occasionally, until mixture begins to bubble and bouillon has dissolved, about 4 minutes.
3. Add diced meat and vegetables, and stir.
4. Reduce heat to low, cover, and simmer for an additional 3 minutes.
5. Remove from heat and let cool. Transfer to airtight storage container and refrigerate or freeze. If refrigerated, serve within 4 days; store up to 3 weeks in the freezer.
6. To serve: Reheat refrigerated stew in a microwave oven on high for 6 minutes, stirring once after 3 minutes. Thaw frozen stew in your microwave, then heat as above. Spoon into lunch box thermos containers.

# Savory Thermos Rice Medley

*If you want to spice up your midday meal, this recipe is sure to please!*

Estimated preparation time: 7 minutes
Estimated cooking time: 13 minutes, including reheating
Makes 4 servings

1. Place rice, tomatoes, and their liquid in a medium nonstick pot. Stir in curry seasoning.
2. Cook uncovered over medium-low heat for 4 minutes, stirring occasionally. Add diced meat and vegetables, stir, reduce heat to low, and simmer uncovered for an additional 3 minutes.
3. Remove from heat and let cool. Transfer to an airtight storage container and refrigerate up to 4 days.
4. To serve: Reheat stew in a microwave oven on high for 6 minutes, stirring once after 3 minutes. Spoon into lunch box thermos containers.

2 cups cooked rice
1 can (15 ounces) diced tomatoes
¼ teaspoon curry seasoning
1½ cups diced cooked chicken, turkey, beef, or pork
1 cup cooked vegetables (leftovers work well)

# Toddler-Sized Meaty Biscuit Bites

1 cup diced cooked chicken,
  turkey, or beef
½ cup cooked vegetables
  (leftovers work well)
2 tablespoons mayonnaise or
  salad dressing
8 prepared biscuits

*These child-sized treats are a great way to sneak vegetables into your toddler's diet.*

Estimated preparation time: 10 minutes
Makes 4 servings

1. Place meat, vegetables, and mayonnaise in food processor and pulse until creamy.
2. Split biscuits in half. Fill with about 1 tablespoon plus 1 teaspoon meat mixture.
3. Place 2 filled biscuits in each of 4 sandwich-sized sealable bags. Refrigerate for up to 4 days, or freeze up to 3 weeks for a quick lunch-box treat.

# Preschool Peanut Butter- and-Fruity Roll-Ups

*Your young child can help you make these easy, nutritious, and delicious snacks, and they're a healthy alternative to peanut butter and jelly sandwiches.*

Estimated preparation time: 10 minutes
Makes 2 servings

1. Place peanut butter and mashed banana in a small bowl and stir until well combined.
2. Spread half the mixture evenly over each tortilla, sprinkle with fruit, and roll tightly. Place in sealable sandwich bags.

3 tablespoons chunky peanut butter
½ ripe banana, mashed
¼ cup chopped dried fruit (such as raisins, apricots, or dates)
2 regular or whole wheat flour tortillas

Lunch-Box Winners　　　　**39**

# Elementary Fajita Pitas

2 tablespoons reduced-fat or
    regular mayonnaise
2 tablespoons mild salsa
1 cup diced cooked chicken,
    turkey, beef, or pork
2 lettuce leaves
1 whole wheat or regular pita,
    cut in half

*Your elementary-school-aged child can make this fun to eat and healthy lunch—and she'll be the envy of the lunchroom.*

Estimated preparation time: 10 minutes
Makes 2 child-sized sandwiches, or 1 adult serving

1. Place mayonnaise and salsa in a small bowl and stir until blended. Stir in diced meat.
2. Place 1 lettuce leaf in each pita pocket, and spoon equal portions of meat mixture into each. Carefully slide pitas into sealable sandwich bags.

# Easy Cheese Pizza Sandwiches

*Nearly everyone loves pizza, and your elementary-school-aged child can make these very quickly.*

2 teaspoons Italian dressing
2 English muffins, split
2 thin slices tomato
2 slices (1 ounce each)
      part-skim mozzarella
      cheese

Estimated preparation time: 8 minutes
Makes 2 child-sized sandwiches, or 1 adult serving

1. Spread 1 teaspoon Italian dressing on each of 2 English muffin halves.
2. Place 1 slice of tomato and 1 slice of cheese over dressing, and top with remaining muffin halves. Carefully wrap sandwiches in plastic wrap or aluminum foil.

# Triple-Decker Turkey Sandwich

2 teaspoons reduced-fat
    mayonnaise
3 slices whole wheat bread
2 thin slices cooked turkey,
    chicken, or beef
2 thin slices tomato
1 fresh spinach leaf

*Older children have larger appetites; your fourth- or fifth-grade child will love making this extra-special sandwich.*

Estimated preparation time: 10 minutes
Makes 1 hearty, low-fat sandwich

1. Spread 1 teaspoon of mayonnaise on top of each of 2 slices of bread.
2. Layer the ingredients: 1 slice bread, 1 slice meat, 1 slice tomato, 1 slice bread, 1 slice meat, 1 slice tomato, spinach leaf, 1 slice bread (without mayonnaise).
3. Slice sandwich in half diagonally, secure with toothpicks, and place in a sealable or fold-over sandwich bag.

# "Oh Bologna" Sandwiches

*An alternative to "plain" sandwiches or burgers, your preteen will enjoy eating this sandwich with homemade tortilla chips and fruit.*

Estimated preparation time: 5 minutes
Makes 2 sandwiches

1. Spread each half of both buns with 1 teaspoon Dijonnaise.
2. Layer each bottom half as follows: 1 slice bologna, 1 slice cheese, 1 slice bologna, 1 slice tomato, 1 lettuce leaf, and bun top. Secure with toothpicks and slide into sealable or fold-over sandwich bags.

2 hamburger-style buns
4 teaspoons Dijonnaise brand creamy mustard
4 slices reduced-fat bologna
2 slices 2%-fat American cheese
2 thin slices tomato
2 small lettuce leaves

# Turkey-Berry Sandwich Treats

4 slices (¼ inch each)
    purchased reduced-fat
    pound cake, toasted
2 tablespoons reduced-fat
    cream cheese spread
2 slices cooked turkey or deli
    turkey lunchmeat
2 tablespoons cranberry sauce

*Healthy, hearty, and delicious, this unusual sandwich is great for using up Thanksgiving leftovers. Try it for a special, post-holiday treat!*

Estimated preparation time: 10 minutes
Makes 2 sandwiches

1. Spread each of 2 toasted pound cake slices with 1 tablespoon cream cheese spread.
2. Place 1 slice turkey and 1 tablespoon cranberry sauce on each, and top with remaining slices of poundcake. Wrap and pack in lunch box.

# Chicken Confetti Pitas

*Go from boring to "boss" with this sandwich alternative. For extra nutrition, purchase whole wheat pita breads.*

2 cups shredded cooked
    chicken
1 cup packaged coleslaw
½ cup reduced-fat shredded
    cheddar cheese
2 teaspoons Thousand Island
    dressing
2 pita breads, cut in half

Estimated preparation time: 8 minutes
Makes 4 pitas, or 2 adult-sized servings

1. Place chicken, vegetables, and cheese in a medium bowl and combine. Drizzle with dressing and toss gently.
2. Spoon mixture into each pita half. Wrap individually, or store in airtight plastic containers.

# Cool, Creamy Ham and Fettuccini Salad

1 tablespoon reduced-fat
    mayonnaise
¼ cup honey-mustard dressing
4 cups cooked fettuccini
    noodles, rinsed and
    drained
¼ cup diced green onions
3 thin slices cooked ham, cut
    into thin strips
1 cup frozen peas and carrots,
    thawed

*On warm days, or when a microwave is not easily available, this creamy salad will win rave reviews from your gang.*

Estimated preparation time: 15 minutes
Estimated refrigeration time: overnight
Makes 4 to 5 servings

1. In a medium bowl, whisk together mayonnaise and honey–mustard dressing. Add remaining ingredients and toss until well combined. Chill overnight.
2. Divide recipe evenly into 4 or 5 one-pint airtight containers. Salad can be safely refrigerated for up to 5 days.

# Happy Burgers and Fries

*Would you like to give your child a special lunch without the extra fat or expense? This recipe will help you make him feel like a lunchtime king!*

Estimated preparation time: 10 minutes
Estimated baking time: 15 minutes
Makes 4 servings

1. Preheat oven to 400 degrees.
2. Lightly coat a nonstick cookie sheet with cooking oil spray. Place vegetarian burgers at each of the four corners of the cookie sheet.
3. Drop frozen shoestring potatoes in a large paper bag, sprinkle with cornstarch and seasoned salt, fold the top of the bag, and shake vigorously. Spread coated potatoes on cookie sheet and mist lightly with cooking oil spray.
4. Slide the cookie sheet onto the center rack of the oven and bake for 15 minutes, or until potatoes are slightly golden.
5. Remove cookie sheet from oven. Assemble sandwiches (hot vegetarian burgers, cheese, and condiments) on whole wheat buns. Serve with slightly cooled fries.

cooking oil spray
4 preformed frozen vegetarian burgers (traditional-style)
1 bag (16 ounces) frozen shoestring potatoes
2 tablespoons cornstarch
1 tablespoon seasoned salt
4 slices 2%-fat American cheese
pickles, mustard, ketchup, to taste
4 whole wheat hamburger-type buns

Note: Consider saving small, inexpensive stickers or toy items throughout the year to include with your Happy Burger meals.

# Nothing But Nachos

½ pound purchased baked
  tortilla chips
1 can (14 ounces) nonfat
  refried beans
1 can (15 ounces) diced
  tomatoes and chilies,
  drained
1 cup reduced-fat shredded
  cheddar cheese

*Nachos are fast, fun, and yummy snacks, but this recipe also makes a balanced, nutritious meal. Your children will want to help you whip it up and gobble it down!*

Estimated preparation time: 10 minutes
Estimated baking time: 10 minutes
Makes 6 to 8 servings

1. Preheat oven to 350 degrees.
2. Arrange tortilla chips along the sides of a large, oven-safe platter. Spoon refried beans into center, and top with tomatoes and cheese. Place the platter on the center rack of the hot oven and bake for 10 minutes, or until cheese melts.
3. Remove from oven, place on hot pad in the center of table, and enjoy.

# 4
# COOK ONCE, EAT THREE TIMES

Specially Seasoned Sirloin
and Vegetables
Last-Minute Beef Stew
Steak and Tomato Baked
Bruschetta
Marvelous Microwave
Meatloaf
Cheesy Meatloaf Burgers
Zesty Meatloaf Salad
Honey-Mustard Roasted
Chicken Breasts
Easy Chicken Tacos
Fuss-Free Chicken Potpie
Casserole
Almond Chicken Cups
Grilled Dilled Salmon
Steaks
Scrambled Egg and
Salmon Frittata

Orange-Baked Catfish
Saucy Seafood Burgers
Oven-Fried Cod
South of the Border Pork
Roast
Zesty Pork and Tortilla Soup
Easy Pork Enchiladas
Pork Chops with Black-
berry Mustard Sauce
Hawaiian Pork Buns
Almost-Traditional Turkey
Dinner
Turkey-and-Stuffing Cus-
tard Cups with Cran-
berry Sauce
Spicy Ground-Turkey
Meatballs
Spaghetti and Spicy Meat-
balls

Today's weekdays and nights are filled with activities and commitments. When you want to make the most of your time in the kitchen, prepare basic dishes that can become the foundation for several evening meals. You can also plan a marathon cooking session on Saturday or Sunday and prepare a week's worth of dinners in a few hours.

This chapter includes simple beginnings and fast encores—the recipe for each main dish is be followed by at least two ideas for the leftovers. Consider cooking two or three main dishes at one time and freezing the items you won't be consuming in a few days. To make even better use of your time, cook one of the main course recipes for Crock-Pots in chapter 5 while you're preparing one or more of these.

Beginning with recipes for beef, you'll find enough ideas for several weeks' worth of menus. Don't forget that many grocery stores today sell partially-prepared items like meatballs and chicken or pork strips, and those foods can be substituted according to your time, budget, and tastes.

One note: Cooked fish doesn't always refreeze well, so the recipes for seafood leftovers have been developed to keep (with care) for a day or two. For safety purposes, no pork recipes call for cold, cooked pork, and all recipes have been designed for well-done main course meats.

# Specially Seasoned Sirloin and Vegetables

*By taking advantage of extra lean cuts of meat, this beefy recipe is less fatty than traditional pot roast and vegetables, without sacrificing taste. Serve this roast with a tossed green salad and dinner rolls.*

Estimated preparation time: 10 minutes
Estimated baking time: 2 to 3 hours
Makes 8 to 10 servings

1. Preheat oven to 325 degrees.
2. Place sirloin in medium to large roasting pan. Spread steak sauce on top, and sprinkle with pepper and basil. Arrange vegetables along sides of meat.
3. Cover tightly with aluminum foil, place in oven, and bake for 2 to 3 hours (about 40 minutes per pound of meat), or until well done.

1 lean sirloin roast (3 to 4 pounds)
2 tablespoons A-1 Bold and Spicy steak sauce
½ teaspoon coarsely ground pepper
2 tablespoons chopped fresh sweet basil
12 small red potatoes, unpeeled
1 package (16 ounces) peeled baby carrots
1 jar (8 ounces) pearl onions, drained

# Last-Minute Beef Stew

2 cups chopped cooked sirloin
from Specially
Seasoned Sirloin and
Vegetables (recipe,
page 51)
1 cup ready-made reduced-fat
beef gravy
remaining potatoes from
Specially Seasoned
Sirloin and Vegetables
(recipe, page 51),
quartered
remaining carrots from
Specially Seasoned
Sirloin and Vegetables
(recipe, page 51), cut
in half
1½ cups frozen peas, thawed

*This is an ideal recipe for a satisfying, last-minute meal from leftovers; it's also great with frozen meatballs in place of the beef (and is no less quick to prepare). When you've made one meal of Specially Seasoned Sirloin and Vegetables, chop 2 cups of leftover meat, make the following recipe, and freeze it for another meal. Serve with sliced French bread or garlic bread.*

Estimated preparation time: 15 minutes
Estimated cooking time: 10 minutes
Makes 4 servings

1. Place all ingredients in medium nonstick pot and stir.
2. Cover and cook over medium heat until gravy begins to boil, stirring occasionally.

# Steak and Tomato Baked Bruschetta

*Looking for a lighter alternative to a steak and vegetable dinner? This is it! Serve with a tossed salad or sliced fruit, and enjoy the compliments.*

Estimated preparation time: 15 minutes
Estimated baking time: 10 minutes
Makes 4 to 5 servings

1. Preheat oven to 400 degrees.
2. Arrange bread slices side by side on nonstick cookie sheet. Brush bread with Italian dressing, sprinkle with chopped sirloin, and add tomato quarters and Parmesan cheese.
3. Bake for 10 minutes and serve immediately.

1 loaf (12 ounces) fresh Italian bread, cut diagonally into 1-inch-thick slices
3 tablespoons fat-free Italian dressing
1½ cups finely diced cooked sirloin from Specially Seasoned Sirloin and Vegetables (recipe, page 51)
½ pint cherry tomatoes, quartered
¼ cup finely shredded Parmesan cheese

# Marvelous Microwave Meatloaf

2 pounds extra-lean ground
        beef
1 egg
1 cup bread crumbs
1 package (1.25 ounces)
        teriyaki seasoning mix
cooking oil spray

*Many of us consider meatloaf a "comfort" food; but few of us have time to prepare it—this recipe whittles your time in the kitchen by half.*

Estimated preparation time: 10 minutes
Estimated cooking time: 32 minutes, including cooling
        time
Makes 8 servings

1. Preheat oven to 375 degrees.
2. Place all ingredients in large mixing bowl, folding and stirring until well combined.
3. Lightly coat $9 \times 4\frac{3}{4}$-inch glass loaf pan with cooking oil spray. Form meat mixture into loaf shape and place in pan.
4. Microwave meatloaf on high for 12 minutes. Transfer to preheated oven and bake for 15 minutes. Remove from oven and allow to cool for 5 minutes before slicing.

· · · · · · · · · · · · · · · ·

Note: Serve this favorite with mashed potatoes, steamed vegetables, and rolls.

· · · · · · · · · · · · · · · ·

# Cheesy Meatloaf Burgers

*What is meatloaf if not hamburger? Try this burger recipe for a quick, lazy-day dinner or lunch on the run.*

Estimated preparation time: 10 minutes
Estimated baking time: 10 to 15 minutes
Makes 4 servings

1. Preheat oven to 325 degrees.
2. Wrap burger buns in foil. Lay meatloaf slices flat on a large piece of foil and wrap.
3. Warm buns and meatloaf in oven for 10 to 15 minutes.
4. Remove buns and meatloaf from oven and assemble burgers. Serve with baked potato chips and fresh fruit.

4 whole wheat burger buns
4 slices leftover meatloaf (from Marvelous Microwave Meatloaf recipe, page 54)
4 slices (1 ounce each) 2%-fat American cheese
4 slices tomato
4 leaves lettuce
ketchup, mustard, pickles, or other condiments, to taste

# Zesty Meatloaf Salad

1 tablespoon oil
dash chile oil
2 slices leftover meatloaf
    (from Marvelous
    Microwave Meatloaf
    recipe, page 54)
1 package (12 ounces) salad
    greens
1 small red onion, sliced into
    thin rings
1 small green pepper, cut into
    thin strips
½ pint cherry tomatoes,
    quartered

*Your family will be surprised by the taste and texture of this delicious entrée. Serve this unusual salad with the dressing of your choice and plenty of fresh bread.*

Estimated preparation time: 15 minutes
Estimated cooking time: 4 minutes
Makes 6 servings

1. Preheat a medium nonstick skillet over medium heat, and add the oils.
2. Sauté the meatloaf slices for 2 minutes on each side. Remove and dice into cubes.
3. Place salad greens in large serving bowl, top with vegetables, and sprinkle with cubed meatloaf.

# Honey-Mustard Roasted Chicken Breasts

*Serve this delicious chicken with steamed rice and vegetables. My picky five-year-old gave this recipe two thumbs up—your children will love it, too!*

cooking oil spray
8 boneless, skinless chicken breasts
1 small red onion, sliced into thin rings
1 teaspoon garlic powder
1 bottle (12 ounces) reduced-fat honey-mustard dressing

Estimated preparation time: 10 minutes
Estimated baking time: ½ hour
Makes 8 servings, or 4 servings if you reserve half the meat

1. Preheat oven to 375 degrees.
2. Lightly coat a $9 \times 13$-inch baking dish with cooking oil spray. Arrange chicken breasts in the bottom, spread onion slices over chicken, and sprinkle with garlic powder. Pour the entire bottle of dressing over all.
3. Cover baking dish with foil and bake for ½ hour, removing foil during last 10 minutes.

. . . . . . . . . . . . . . . . .

Note: Here's a time-saving tip: When the cooked chicken has cooled enough to be handled, dice or slice half the total yield for use in other recipes—it will keep in the refrigerator for up to 3 days in an airtight container.

. . . . . . . . . . . . . . . . .

# Easy Chicken Tacos

2 cups diced chicken meat
    from leftovers
1 can (15¼ ounces)
    Del Monte Fiesta corn
1 cup salsa
12 packaged taco shells
1 cup reduced-fat shredded
    cheddar cheese

*This tasty, colorful alternative to fast-food tacos is as fun to make as it is to eat.*

Estimated preparation time: 10 minutes
Estimated cooking time: 10 minutes
Makes 6 servings

1. Place chicken, corn, and salsa in medium pot and heat over low heat, stirring occasionally, until hot.
2. Spoon the heated filling into prepared taco shells, sprinkle with cheese, and serve.

# Fuss-Free Chicken Potpie Casserole

*At the end of a long, tiring day nothing could be simpler than this low-fat recipe using leftover chicken.*

Estimated preparation time: 15 minutes
Estimated baking time: 20 minutes
Makes 8 servings

1. Preheat oven to 375 degrees.
2. Place the chicken, mixed vegetables, soup, and cheese in a large mixing bowl and stir until well combined.
3. Lightly coat a $9 \times 13$-inch baking dish with cooking oil spray. Open 1 can crescent rolls, unroll dough sheet (do *not* separate the rolls), and press into bottom of baking dish. Spoon meat and vegetable mixture onto the dough and spread evenly.
4. Open remaining can of dough, unroll, place on top of meat and vegetable mixture, and press. Pinch edges of dough to seal.
5. Bake for 20 minutes, or until dough is cooked and filling is bubbly.

$1\frac{1}{2}$ cups diced cooked chicken breast
1 can (15 ounces) mixed vegetables, drained
1 can ($10\frac{3}{4}$ ounces) reduced-fat cream of mushroom soup
$\frac{1}{2}$ cup fat-free shredded cheddar cheese
cooking oil spray
2 cans reduced-fat crescent rolls

# Almond Chicken Cups

½ cup chopped red bell
    pepper
½ cup chopped onion
2 cups chopped cooked
    chicken (leftovers
    work well)
⅔ cup bottled sweet and sour
    sauce
½ cup whole almonds
6 flour tortillas (6 inch)

*These attractive, tasty "cups" will win over anyone who normally turns down "leftovers."*

Estimated preparation time: 10 minutes
Estimated baking time: 12 to 15 minutes, including cooling time
Makes 12 chicken cups

1. Preheat oven to 400 degrees.
2. Place pepper, onion, chicken, sweet and sour sauce, and almonds in a medium bowl. Toss gently to combine.
3. Cover tortillas with a damp paper towel and microwave on high for 30 seconds to soften.
4. Cut each tortilla in half. Place each half in a paper-lined muffin tin. Fill each tortilla with ¼ cup chicken mixture.
5. Bake for 8 to 10 minutes, until chicken mixture is hot. Remove from oven and allow to cool for 5 minutes before serving.

# Grilled Dilled Salmon Steaks

*This salmon is great with a simple side dish of steamed rice and vegetables. If you have any leftover salmon, flake it and use it to make the Scrambled Egg and Salmon Frittata that follows.*

4 small salmon steaks
    (¼ pound each)
2 tablespoons olive oil
2 tablespoons freshly
    squeezed lemon juice
2 teaspoons chopped fresh dill
    weed

Estimated preparation time: 5 minutes
Estimated cooking time: 10 to 14 minutes
Makes 4 servings

1. Preheat the broiler or grill.
2. Rinse salmon steaks and pat dry.
3. Mix oil, lemon juice, and dill in a small bowl and stir briskly to combine. Brush over steaks.
4. Grill or broil salmon, turning once, until cooked through (about 5 to 7 minutes a side). Serve immediately.

# Scrambled Egg and Salmon Frittata

2 tablespoons light canola oil
3 cups frozen hash brown
    potatoes, thawed
8 eggs, or 4 containers egg
    substitute, thawed
¾ cup nonfat sour cream
2 teaspoons chopped chives
1 cup flaked, cooked salmon
    (from Grilled Dilled
    Salmon Steaks recipe,
    page 61)

*Simple to prepare and ready in twenty minutes or less, this dinner is a lifesaver on busy nights.*

Estimated preparation time: 10 minutes
Estimated cooking time: 7 to 10 minutes
Makes 8 servings

1. Preheat large nonstick skillet over medium heat. Add canola oil, and spread hash brown potatoes evenly over bottom of pan.
2. Place eggs, sour cream, and chives in medium bowl and whisk together. Stir in flaked salmon.
3. Pour egg mixture over potatoes, cover, reduce heat to low, and simmer for 7 to 10 minutes.
4. Slide frittata onto a serving dish, cut into wedges, and serve.

# Orange-Baked Catfish

*Tender, tangy, and low in fat, this dish proves that fish doesn't need to be fried in order to be delicious. Serve it with wild rice and salad for a truly special treat your family will love.*

$\frac{1}{4}$ cup frozen orange juice
    concentrate, thawed
1 tablespoon light canola oil
2 tablespoons lemon juice
1 teaspoon minced garlic
$\frac{1}{8}$ teaspoon coarsely ground
    pepper
4 to 6 catfish fillets

Estimated preparation time: 5 minutes
Estimated baking time: 12 to 15 minutes
Makes 4 to 6 servings

1. Preheat oven to 400 degrees.
2. Place orange juice, oil, lemon juice, garlic, and pepper in small bowl. Stir to combine.
3. Arrange fish fillets in the bottom of nonstick $9 \times 13$-inch baking pan and pour sauce over fish.
4. Place fish on the center rack of the oven and bake for 12 to 15 minutes.

# Saucy Seafood Burgers

2 cups leftover cooked
    seafood, flaked
2 green onions, chopped fine
1 egg
¾ cup dried bread crumbs
1 tablespoon prepared
    mustard
½ teaspoon prepared
    horseradish
4 whole wheat hamburger-
    style buns

*Leftover fish doesn't need to be thrown away. Try these burgers with oven "fries" and fresh fruit.*

Estimated preparation time: 10 minutes
Estimated baking time: 12 minutes
Makes 4 servings

1. Preheat oven to 400 degrees.
2. In medium bowl, blend seafood, onion, egg, bread crumbs, mustard, and horseradish until well combined. Shape into 4 equal patties.
3. Place patties on a nonstick cookie sheet and bake for 12 minutes. Remove from oven, place on burger buns, and garnish to taste.

# Oven-Fried Cod

*As a child, I looked forward to the all-you-can-eat fish fry at Fass Brothers restaurant. I can achieve the same results today with much less fat, and you can, too.*

Estimated preparation time: 15 minutes
Estimated baking time: 10 to 12 minutes
Makes 6 servings

2 tablespoons reduced-fat mayonnaise
2 tablespoons fat-free honey-mustard dressing
1 teaspoon lemon juice
$\frac{2}{3}$ cup dried bread crumbs
$\frac{1}{3}$ cup finely crushed corn flakes
6 cod fillets, thawed if frozen

1. Preheat the oven to 425 degrees.
2. Thoroughly combine mayonnaise, dressing, and lemon juice in a pie tin. Combine bread crumbs and crushed corn flakes in a second pie tin.
3. Dredge cod fillets first in wet ingredients, and then in dry ingredients. Be sure to coat fillets completely with each dredge.
4. Place on nonstick baking sheet and bake for 10 to 12 minutes.

Note: Serve these fillets with oven fries and coleslaw.

# South of the Border Pork Roast

1 lean pork roast (3 to 4
       pounds)
⅓ cup dry red wine
¼ cup fat-free Italian dressing
1 teaspoon minced garlic
2 tablespoons chili powder
¼ teaspoon ground cumin

*No one will believe that this spicy, savory roast was prepared using only five ingredients!*

Estimated preparation time: 5 minutes
Estimated baking time: 2 to 3 hours
Makes 8 to 10 servings

1. Preheat oven to 350 degrees.
2. Place pork in medium roasting pan.
3. Whisk together the remaining ingredients in a small bowl and pour over the meat.
4. Bake for 2 to 3 hours, or until well done.

................

Note: Serve this flavorful roast with rice, beans, and a tossed salad.

................

# Zesty Pork and Tortilla Soup

*Would you like a "South of the Border," balanced dinner that's ready to serve before the evening news ends? Then you'll love this one-pot meal!*

Estimated preparation time: 10 minutes
Estimated cooking time: 10 minutes
Makes 6 servings

1. Place all ingredients except tortilla strips into medium nonstick pot and bring to a low boil.
2. Reduce heat to low, stir in tortilla strips, and simmer for 2 to 3 minutes.

1 can (15 ounces) diced tomatoes
1 can (8 ounces) tomato sauce
1 can (4 ounces) diced green chilies
¼ cup chopped cilantro
2 cups shredded cooked pork (from South of the Border Pork Roast recipe, page 66)
3 cups water
6 corn tortillas (6 inch), cut into strips

# Easy Pork Enchiladas

2 cups shredded cooked pork
2 green onions, diced
½ cup picante sauce
cooking oil spray
6 corn tortillas (6 inch)
1 cup reduced-fat shredded
    cheddar cheese

*Picky eaters will gobble up these enchiladas with glee; serve them with rice, nonfat refried beans, and a tossed salad.*

Estimated preparation time: 15 minutes
Estimated baking time: 10 minutes
Makes 6 servings

1. Preheat oven to 350 degrees.
2. Place pork, onions, and ¼ cup picante sauce in small bowl and combine.
3. Lightly coat both sides of each corn tortilla with cooking oil spray. Layer between paper towels and microwave for 30 seconds.
4. Spoon meat mixture into center of each tortilla, roll enchilada-style, and place seam-side down in nonstick $9 \times 13$-inch baking dish. Spoon remaining picante sauce over enchiladas and top with shredded cheddar cheese.
5. Bake for 10 minutes.

# Pork Chops with Blackberry Mustard Sauce

*These sweet and tangy pork chops can be used in a variety of unusual recipes. Shred leftover meat and serve on burger buns with sliced, golden tomatoes, and your family will feel they're being treated to gourmet fare!*

6 lean pork sirloin or loin chops
1 cup fresh blackberries
¼ cup Dijon mustard
3 tablespoons honey
1 tablespoon red wine vinegar
1 teaspoon thyme
¼ teaspoon salt
¼ teaspoon pepper

Estimated preparation time: 5 minutes
Estimated baking time: 45 minutes
Makes 6 servings

1. Preheat oven to 400 degrees.
2. Arrange pork chops in the bottom of 9 × 13-inch baking pan.
3. Place the remaining ingredients in blender and pulse until smooth. Pour over meat.
4. Cover baking dish with foil and bake for 45 minutes.

# Hawaiian Pork Buns

1 can (15 ounces) refrigerated
　　pizza dough
2 cup diced cooked pork
$\frac{1}{4}$ cup frozen orange juice
　　concentrate, thawed
$\frac{1}{4}$ cup crushed pineapple
1 tablespoon minced cilantro

*Use the leftover meat from the Pork Chops with Blackberry Mustard Sauce recipe (page 69) for extra zing in this quick, easy dish.*

Estimated preparation time: 10 minutes
Estimated baking time: 20 minutes
Makes 6 servings

1. Preheat oven to 375 degrees.
2. Unroll refrigerated pizza dough. Slice in half lengthwise and in thirds horizontally to form 6 squares. Press each square of dough to flatten.
3. Combine remaining ingredients in small bowl, tossing to coat pork thoroughly.
4. Using a slotted spoon, drop one-sixth of the meat mixture into the center of each square, fold up corners, and pinch to seal.
5. Place buns on a nonstick baking sheet and bake for 20 minutes or until golden brown.

# Almost-Traditional Turkey Dinner

*Turkey dinners remind us of hearth and home but are time consuming and messy to prepare. This is a faster, simpler alternative with all the flavor your family expects.*

Estimated preparation time: 15 minutes
Estimated baking time: 25 minutes
Makes 6 servings

1. Preheat the oven to 350 degrees.
2. Heat medium nonstick skillet over medium heat. Add oil, and quickly brown both sides of each turkey slice. Set aside.
3. Place chicken flavored rice mix, cornbread cubes, and hot water in large mixing bowl. Toss to combine, and allow to sit for 2 minutes. Add the dried cranberries and chopped spinach, and toss. Spread mixture evenly in the bottom of nonstick $9 \times 13$-inch baking dish. Arrange browned turkey slices over stuffing, and the pour entire jar of gravy over all.
4. Bake for 25 minutes, until heated through.

• • • • • • • • • • • • • •

Note: A double-leftover bonanza: Serve this leftover turkey-day meal with salad and rolls. Then use the leftovers from this meal to make Turkey-and-Stuffing Custard Cups with Cranberry Sauce (page 72).

• • • • • • • • • • • • • •

2 tablespoons light canola oil
6 fresh turkey breast slices
1 package (6.9 ounces) chicken flavor rice mix (such as Rice-A-Roni brand)
3 cups cornbread cubes for stuffing
3 cups hot water
1 cup dried cranberries
4 leaves fresh spinach, chopped fine, or 1 cup frozen chopped spinach, thawed and patted dry
1 jar (16 ounces) reduced-fat turkey gravy

# Turkey-and-Stuffing Custard Cups with Cranberry Sauce

2 cups diced cooked turkey breast
2 cups leftover stuffing, slightly warmed (not hot)
1 container (4 ounces) egg substitute, thawed, or two eggs, beaten
cooking oil spray
1 cup canned jellied cranberry sauce
6 large lettuce leaves

*These meal-in-a-muffin custard cups are portable, packable, and ideal for last minute dinners or picnics. Although small, they're very rich—they can also be individually wrapped and frozen for quick lunchtime fare.*

Estimated preparation time: 10 minutes
Estimated baking time: 12 minutes
Makes 6 servings

1. Preheat the oven to 400 degrees.
2. Combine turkey, stuffing, and eggs or egg substitute in medium bowl.
3. Lightly coat muffin tin with cooking oil spray. Spoon turkey and stuffing mixture into prepared muffin cups. Place on center rack of the oven and bake for 12 minutes.
4. Place the jellied cranberry sauce in glass measuring cup and microwave on high for 1 minute. Stir, and microwave for an additional 30 seconds (the sauce will be very hot).
5. Arrange lettuce leaves on each dinner plate. Place 2 turkey-and-stuffing custard cups on each leaf, and drizzle with cranberry sauce.

# Spicy Ground-Turkey Meatballs

*You can purchase prepared meatballs in the freezer section of your grocery store, yet budget-conscious cooks will appreciate the savings these lower-fat meatballs provide.*

1 pound ground turkey
¼ cup diced green pepper (fresh or frozen)
¼ cup diced onions (fresh or frozen)
¼ teaspoon chili powder
1 egg
¾ cup Italian-seasoned bread crumbs
2 tablespoons light canola oil
1 cup water

Estimated preparation time: 5 minutes
Estimated cooking time: 15 minutes
Makes approximately 24 meatballs

1. Preheat large nonstick skillet over medium-low heat.
2. Place ground turkey, green pepper, and onions in medium bowl, and combine. Sprinkle with chili powder, add egg and seasoned bread crumbs, and mix well. Form into 1-inch balls.
3. Add oil to skillet and brown meatballs over medium-low heat, turning carefully. When meatballs have browned, add water and simmer until all liquid has evaporated (about 10 minutes).

· · · · · · · · · · · · · · · ·

Note: When these meatballs have cooled slightly, place them in zip-top freezer bags and freeze for up to 2 months. Use them in other recipes, such as Spaghetti and Spicy Meatballs (page 74).

· · · · · · · · · · · · · · · ·

# Spaghetti and Spicy Meatballs

1 pound spaghetti, cooked
1 jar (28 ounces) chunky
    spaghetti sauce
12 Spicy Ground-Turkey
    Meatballs (recipe,
    page 73)

*The microwave oven makes this classic even easier, and you can add fresh herbs, mushrooms, or other favorites according to your family's tastes.*

Estimated preparation time: 5 minutes
Estimated cooking time: 10 minutes
Makes 6 generous servings

1. Place the spaghetti noodles in a large, microwavable serving bowl. Pour the spaghetti sauce over the pasta and arrange the meatballs on top.
2. Cover with plastic wrap and microwave on medium-high for 10 minutes.

Note: Serve with tossed salad and garlic bread.

# 5
# DINNER

Simply Creamy Chicken-Vegetable Soup
Two-Step Pepperoni Minestrone
Easy Corn Bisque
Really Easy Roast Beef
Three-Star Chuck Roast
Really Simple Roasted Chicken
Caribbean One-Pot Chicken
Year-Round BBQ Chicken
Favorite Braised Lamb Chops
Power-Dinner Pork Roast
Hearty Ham and Apples
Crowd-Pleasing Bratwurst
Shrimp and Veggie Empanadas

In-a-Flash Chicken Empanadas
Winning Beef and Vegetables
Creamy Beef Stroganoff
Creamy Ham and Vegetables
Golden Ham and Pasta Salad
Ham and Cheese Burritos
Basic Bread Machine Mix
Savory Herbed Bread
Spicy Pepper Bread
Sour Cream and Chives Bread
Breakfast Bread
Hearty Oat Bread

If you regularly put in long hours at work, battle rush-hour traffic, or act as taxi driver for multiple weekday-evening events, you know how important it is to have a collection of "ready when you are" dinner recipes on hand. That's what this chapter is all about—providing you with a little kitchen magic.

Each of the soup recipes listed can be assembled in the morning and heated quickly in the evening. The Crock-Pot entrées go together in minutes and simmer happily while you're busy with the rest of your life. Or, when the pantry is almost bare, grab a few supermarket ingredients on your way home to make a meal in minutes.

If you love freshly baked breads but don't feel you have the time to make them, you'll love the simple bread machine recipes—and they can be served with most of the dinners in this cookbook. With all of the ideas on the following pages, you'll be ready to unwind and enjoy a waiting meal at the end of your busy day.

# Simply Creamy Chicken-Vegetable Soup

*A handful of ingredients, one pot, three minutes of preparation time, and ten minutes to serve. What could be easier?*

Estimated preparation time: 3 minutes
Estimated cooking time: 10 minutes
Makes 8 servings

1. Place all ingredients in medium nonstick pot. Cook over medium heat, stirring occasionally.
2. When soup begins to bubble, remove from heat and serve.

· · · · · · · · · · · · · · · ·

Note: Serve this soup with fresh bread or reduced-fat biscuits.

· · · · · · · · · · · · · · · ·

2 cups diced cooked chicken (leftovers work well)
1 cup cooked rice (leftovers work well)
1 can (15 ounces) mixed vegetables, drained
1 can (15 ounces) cream-style corn
1 cup water
salt and pepper, to taste

# Two-Step Pepperoni Minestrone

1 can (15 ounces) Italian-style
diced tomatoes
1 can (8 ounces) tomato sauce
1 can (16 ounces) red kidney
beans, drained
2 cups packaged coleslaw
1 package (3.5 ounces)
pepperoni slices,
halved
4 cups water
½ cup uncooked bow-tie pasta

*Pepperoni soup? It's simple, zesty, and sure to please the pickiest eaters.*

Estimated preparation time: 10 minutes
Estimated cooking time: 10 minutes
Makes 6 servings

1. Combine canned tomatoes, tomato sauce, and kidney beans in medium nonstick pot. Stir. Add vegetables and pepperoni, and stir again. Add water and pasta.
2. Bring soup to low boil over medium heat, reduce heat to low, cover, and simmer for 5 minutes.

..................

Note: Serve with garlic toast and fresh fruit.

..................

# Easy Corn Bisque

*For everyone who loves traditional corn chowder (but doesn't want the traditional fat and calories), this bisque is a delicious surprise.*

Estimated preparation time: 5 minutes
Estimated cooking time: 12 minutes, including setting time
Makes 6 servings

1. Place sweet potatoes, corn, onion, garlic, coriander, and sage into blender and pulse until smooth. Continue, or refrigerate until ready to use.
2. Pour pureed corn mixture into a medium nonstick pot. Heat on low until mixture begins to bubble, stirring occasionally. Remove from heat and cool for 2 minutes.
3. Stir in sour cream and serve.

1 can (16 ounces) sweet potatoes, drained
2 cans (15 ounces each) cream-style corn
½ cup diced onion (fresh or frozen)
1 teaspoon minced garlic
½ teaspoon coriander
½ teaspoon sage
1 cup nonfat sour cream

# Really Easy Roast Beef

1 lean beef roast (2 or 3 pounds), frozen or partially frozen (any cut, shaped to fit your Crock-Pot)

1 pound small, unpeeled red potatoes

1 package (16 ounces) peeled fresh baby carrots

½ pound fresh snap peas in pods (if available)

1 can (15 ounces) French onion soup

½ cup water

*Five minutes preparation in the morning is all it takes for this "down home" recipe that's ready when you are. Serve with fresh bread and salad if desired.*

Estimated preparation time: 5 minutes
Estimated cooking time: 8 to 10 hours
Makes 8 servings

1. Place roast in the bottom of Crock-Pot and arrange potatoes, carrots, and peas around meat. Pour the can of soup and water over meat and vegetables.
2. Cover and cook on low for 8 to 10 hours.

# Three-Star Chuck Roast

*Sometimes the simpler the recipe, the better the meal; such is the case with this family favorite. You don't need fancy seasonings to get stellar reviews at dinner time.*

1 boneless chuck roast
    (3 pounds)
$\frac{1}{2}$ teaspoon salt
$\frac{1}{2}$ teaspoon coarsely ground
    pepper
$\frac{1}{4}$ teaspoon garlic powder
$\frac{1}{2}$ cup chopped onion (fresh
    or frozen)

Estimated preparation time: 3 minutes
Estimated cooking time: 7 to 8 hours
Makes 8 servings

1. Place roast in Crock-Pot and sprinkle with salt, pepper, garlic powder, and onion.
2. Cover and cook on low for 7 to 8 hours.

# Really Simple Roasted Chicken

1 roasting chicken (4 to 5 pounds)
½ teaspoon salt
½ teaspoon coarsely ground pepper
½ teaspoon dried thyme
¼ teaspoon garlic powder

*Chicken can be prepared safely in a slow cooker. Be sure to drain and discard the drippings, and store any leftover chicken in a clean container in the refrigerator.*

Estimated preparation time: 5 minutes
Estimated cooking time: 7 to 8 hours
Makes 4½ cups cooked chicken, or serves 8

1. Remove giblets from chicken. Reserve for later use (boil giblets in a small amount of water until cooked, and freeze or refrigerate) or discard.
2. Rinse chicken in cold water, drain, and place breast side up in the Crock-Pot. Sprinkle with salt, pepper, thyme, and garlic powder.
3. Cover and cook on low for 7 to 8 hours.

# Caribbean One-Pot Chicken

*For chicken with a little more zing, prepare this recipe for your gang. Use any leftovers in a simple, savory salad.*

6 boneless, skinless chicken breasts
1 can (15 ounces) mandarin oranges, drained
1 red onion, thinly sliced
1 cup orange juice
¼ teaspoon garlic powder
½ teaspoon ground ginger

Estimated preparation time: 5 minutes
Estimated cooking time: 5 to 8 hours
Makes 6 servings

1. Arrange chicken breasts in the bottom of Crock-Pot and top with oranges and onion slices. Pour orange juice over all, and sprinkle with garlic powder and ginger.
2. Cover and cook on low for 5 to 8 hours.

# Year-Round BBQ Chicken

2 pounds frozen chicken thighs (to reduce fat, purchase boneless, skinless variety)
½ cup Kentucky Bourbon
½ cup A-1 Bold and Spicy steak sauce
¼ teaspoon Chinese hot mustard
1 tablespoon vinegar
2 tablespoons honey
½ cup warm water
3 bell peppers (1 each red, yellow, and green) sliced (optional)

*Summer months aren't the only time of year you can enjoy barbecued chicken. This recipe also works well with beef or pork ribs.*

Estimated preparation time: 5 minutes
Estimated cooking time: 6 to 8 hours
Makes 6 servings

1. Allow chicken thighs to partially thaw, and arrange in the bottom of a Crock-Pot.
2. Place remaining ingredients except peppers in large glass measuring cup or small glass bowl. Whisk together until well blended, then pour over the chicken.
3. Cover and cook on low for 6 to 8 hours. If desired, add peppers during the last hour of cooking.

Note: Serve with rice, salad, and rolls.

# Favorite Braised Lamb Chops

*If you think lamb dishes are too complicated to tackle in your kitchen, you'll be surprised at how easy this is to prepare.*

Estimated preparation time: 7 minutes
Estimated cooking time: 6 to 8 hours
Makes 6 to 8 servings

1. Arrange the lamb chops in the bottom of a Crock-Pot and cover with the onion slices.
2. Place remaining ingredients except potatoes in a small bowl and whisk until well blended. Pour over meat and onions.
3. Cover and cook on low for 6 to 8 hours. If desired, add potatoes during the last hour of cooking, increasing setting temperature to high.

. . . . . . . . . . . . . . . . .

Note: Serve with salad and fresh bread.

. . . . . . . . . . . . . . . . .

2 to 3 pounds lean lamb chops
1 small sweet onion, thinly sliced
½ cup Heinz 57 sauce
¼ cup reduced-sodium soy sauce
2 teaspoons chopped fresh rosemary (if using the dry variety, reduce to 1 teaspoon and crush to release flavor)
½ teaspoon minced garlic
½ cup warm water
8 small, unpeeled red potatoes (optional)

# Power-Dinner Pork Roast

1 boneless pork roast or
    tenderloin (3 to 4
    pounds)
⅔ cup fat-free Italian dressing
½ teaspoon dried rosemary

*Three ingredients and three minutes' preparation time make one powerful meal for busy cooks everywhere.*

Estimated preparation time: 3 minutes
Estimated cooking time: 7 to 8 hours
Makes 8 servings

1. Place pork roast in Crock-Pot. Pour Italian dressing over meat, and sprinkle with rosemary.
2. Cover and cook on low for 7 to 8 hours.

# Hearty Ham and Apples

*This recipe has won rave reviews with my family and friends—try it and take your own bows.*

Estimated preparation time: 5 minutes
Estimated cooking time: 5 to 8 hours
Makes 6 to 8 servings

1 turkey ham (3 pounds)
1 can (16 ounces) light apple
    pie filling
¼ teaspoon ground ginger
¼ teaspoon cinnamon

1. Place ham in Crock-Pot. Pour apple pie filling over ham, and sprinkle with ginger and cinnamon.
2. Cover and cook on low for 5 to 8 hours.

# Crowd-Pleasing Bratwurst

12 fresh bratwurst (about 3
  pounds)
1 medium sweet onion,
  quartered
1 medium red onion,
  quartered
1 red, 1, green, and 1 yellow
  bell pepper, cored,
  seeded, and sliced into
  strips
1 can (12 ounces) beer
½ cup water
12 hamburger-style buns

*Looking for the perfect recipe for your tailgate picnic? This is it!*

Estimated preparation time: 10 minutes
Estimated cooking time: 6 to 8 hours
Makes 10 to 12 servings

1. Arrange bratwurst and vegetables in bottom of Crock-Pot, and cover with beer and water.
2. Cover and simmer on low for 6 to 8 hours. Discard broth.
3. Serve on hamburger buns.

Note: Accompany this dish with creamy potato salad and salad greens.

# Shrimp and Veggie Empanadas

*Supermarket staples make this recipe a mom's best friend, and the kids love it, too!*

Estimated preparation time: 5 minutes
Estimated baking time: 20 minutes
Makes 4 servings (2 large empanadas)

1. Preheat oven to 400 degrees.
2. Combine rice, sour cream, and cheese in a large mixing bowl. Gently stir in tomato, broccoli, and shrimp.
3. Spoon half the rice mixture onto the center of each pie crust. Gently fold crust to form half-moon shape, then press with a fork to seal edges.
4. Place empanadas on a nonstick cookie sheet, and bake for 20 minutes, or until golden brown. Cut in half and serve.

2 cups cooked rice (leftovers work well)
½ cup nonfat sour cream
½ cup shredded reduced-fat cheddar cheese
1 medium tomato, diced fine
1 cup cooked chopped broccoli (leftovers work well)
1 package (6 ounces) frozen cooked shrimp, partially thawed
1 package (15 ounces) refrigerated unbaked pie crust (2 crusts)

# In-a-Flash Chicken Empanadas

2 cups diced cooked chicken (leftovers or packaged, frozen)
1 can (15 ounces) whole-kernel corn, drained
¼ cup diced green pepper (fresh or frozen)
¾ cup chunky salsa
1 package (15 ounces) refrigerated unbaked pie crust (2 crusts)
1 cup shredded reduced-fat cheddar cheese

*Because you just can't have too many empanada recipes . . .*

Estimated preparation time: 5 minutes
Estimated baking time: 20 minutes
Makes 4 servings (2 large empanadas)

1. Preheat oven to 400 degrees.
2. Combine chicken, corn, pepper, and salsa in a large mixing bowl.
3. Spoon half the mixture onto each pie crust, and sprinkle half the cheese over the mixture. Gently fold crust to form half-moon shape, then press with a fork to seal edges.
4. Place empanadas on an ungreased cookie sheet and bake for 20 minutes, or until golden brown. Cut in half and serve.

# Winning Beef and Vegetables

*My youngest is suspicious of most entrées that contain a lot of vegetables, but he eats this without complaint.*

Estimated preparation time: 5 minutes
Estimated cooking time: 15 minutes
Makes 6 servings

1 tablespoon canola oil
½ cup chopped onion (fresh or frozen)
2 cups chopped cooked beef (from leftovers)
1 can (15 ounces) diced tomatoes
1 can (15 ounces) mixed vegetables, drained

1. Preheat nonstick skillet over medium heat.
2. Add oil and sauté onions, stirring frequently. Add beef, tomatoes, and vegetables and stir.
3. Reduce heat to low and simmer for 10 minutes.

Note: Serve over cooked pasta or rice for success with your picky eaters.

# Creamy Beef Stroganoff

2 cups diced cooked beef
    (from leftovers)
1 can (10.75 ounces) reduced-
    fat cream of
    mushroom soup
1 can (15 ounces) mixed peas
    and carrots, drained
1 cup sliced fresh mushrooms
1 package (16 ounces) egg
    noodles, cooked and
    drained

*Beef Stroganoff used to take hours to prepare, but not any more!*

Estimated preparation time: 5 minutes
Estimated cooking time: 7 to 8 minutes
Makes 6 to 8 servings

1. Place beef, soup, peas and carrots, and mushrooms in microwavable casserole dish.
2. Microwave for 5 minutes on high, then stir. Microwave for an additional 2 to 3 minutes on high, and stir again.
3. Serve over noodles.

# Creamy Ham and Vegetables

*This is a great way to use up leftover ham. Serve over cooked rice or biscuits.*

Estimated preparation time: 4 minutes
Estimated cooking time: 7 minutes
Makes 6 servings

1. Place all ingredients in microwavable casserole dish.
2. Microwave on high for 3 minutes, then stir. Microwave for an additional 3 to 4 minutes on high, and stir again.

2 cups diced cooked ham (leftovers work well)
1 can (10.75 ounces) condensed cream of celery soup
$\frac{1}{3}$ cup skim milk
1 can (15-ounces) mixed vegetables, drained
$\frac{1}{4}$ teaspoon coarsely ground pepper

# Golden Ham and Pasta Salad

1 package (12 ounces) spiral
   pasta, cooked and
   drained
2 cups diced cooked ham
   (leftovers work well)
1 can (8 ounces) French-style
   green beans, drained
1 can (8 ounces) sliced
   carrots, drained
½ cup fat-free honey-mustard
   salad dressing
¼ cup golden raisins

*Your children will love the sweet, tangy flavor and golden raisins in this special salad.*

Estimated preparation time: 5 minutes
Estimated cooking time: 8 minutes (pasta)
Estimated refrigeration time: 20 minutes
Makes 6 servings

**1.** Place all ingredients in large salad bowl and toss to combine. Chill before serving.

# Ham and Cheese Burritos

*Try these for breakfast, brunch, lunch, dinner, or snacks . . . they're so easy and yummy, it's hard to limit them to one meal.*

1½ cups diced cooked ham (leftovers work well)
1 cup reduced-fat shredded cheddar cheese
2 green onions, finely chopped
6 flour tortillas (8 inch)

Estimated preparation time: 5 minutes
Estimated baking time: 10 minutes
Makes 6 servings

1. Preheat oven to 350 degrees.
2. Place diced ham, cheese, and onions in medium bowl and toss to combine.
3. Spoon mixture into center of tortillas and fold burrito style.
4. Arrange burritos on nonstick cookie sheet and bake for 10 minutes, until cheese is melted.

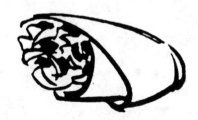

# Basic Bread Machine Mix

3 cups flour
2 tablespoons sugar
1 tablespoon powdered skim
    milk
1½ teaspoons salt
2¼ teaspoons bread machine
    yeast

*I adore my bread machine, but can't always afford the prices of fancy bread mixes. This basic recipe can be adapted many, many ways, as you'll see in the recipes that follow.*

Estimated preparation time: 5 minutes
Makes 3 cups bread mix, enough for 1 loaf (1½ pounds)

1. Combine all ingredients.
2. Store in an airtight container and refrigerate for up to 3 weeks.

# Savory Herbed Bread

*I prefer to use fresh herbs whenever possible, but slightly crushed dried herbs work well in this recipe.*

Estimated preparation time: 5 minutes
Estimated baking time: varies according to bread
   machine
Makes 12 slices (1½-pound loaf)

1 cup warm water
Basic Bread Machine Mix
   (recipe, page 96)
1 tablespoon reduced-fat
   margarine
1 tablespoon fat-free grated
   Parmesan cheese
½ teaspoon thyme
½ teaspoon oregano

1. Pour warm water into bread machine. Add bread mix and remaining ingredients.
2. Select basic/white cycle on machine and press start.
3. Remove bread from pan while still warm. Allow to cool, then slice and serve.

# Spicy Pepper Bread

1 cup warm water
Basic Bread Machine Mix
    (recipe, page 96)
2 tablespoons canola oil
2 tablespoons diced red
    pepper (fresh, frozen,
    or canned)
1 teaspoon lemon pepper
    seasoning

*My recipe testers raved about this adaptation for the basic bread mix recipe; it'll be a hit in your home, too.*

Estimated preparation time: 5 minutes
Estimated baking time: varies according to bread
    machine
Makes 12 slices (1½-pound loaf)

1. Pour warm water into bread machine. Add bread mix and remaining ingredients.
2. Select basic/white cycle on machine and press start.
3. Remove bread from pan while still warm. Allow to cool, then slice and serve.

# Sour Cream and Chives Bread

*Even if you never thought of sour cream and chives in a bread recipe before, you'll be convinced that this combination works when you try it.*

Estimated preparation time: 5 minutes
Estimated baking time: varies according to bread machine
Makes 12 slices (1½-pound loaf)

1 cup warm water
Basic Bread Machine Mix
    (recipe, page 96)
¼ cup instant mashed potato
    flakes
⅓ cup fat-free sour cream
1 tablespoon chopped fresh
    chives

1. Pour warm water into bread machine. Add bread mix and remaining ingredients.
2. Select basic/white cycle on machine and press start.
3. Remove bread from pan while still warm. Allow to cool, then slice and serve.

# Breakfast Bread

1 cup warm water
¼ cup frozen orange juice
    concentrate, thawed
Basic Bread Machine Mix
    (recipe, page 96)
¾ cup fat-free granola
2 tablespoons nonfat plain
    yogurt

*I have baked this many times by setting the bread machine timer to have warm bread ready when the alarm clock interrupts my slumber—it's delicious!*

Estimated preparation time: 5 minutes
Estimated baking time: varies according to bread machine
Makes 12 slices (1½-pound loaf)

1. Pour warm water into bread machine.
2. Pour thawed frozen orange juice concentrate into glass measuring cup. Microwave on medium for 20 seconds.
3. Add warm orange juice to the water in the bread machine. Add bread mix and remaining ingredients.
4. Select sweet cycle on machine and press start.
5. Remove bread from pan while still warm. Allow to cool, then slice and serve.

# Hearty Oat Bread

*Oats add body and texture to this special winter adaptation (but you can enjoy it any time of year).*

Estimated preparation time: 5 minutes

Estimated baking time: varies according to bread machine

Makes 12 slices (1½-pound loaf)

1¼ cups warm water
Basic Bread Machine Mix (recipe, page 96)
½ cup old fashioned oats
2 tablespoons dark brown sugar
2 tablespoons nonfat plain yogurt

1. Pour warm water into bread machine. Add bread mix and remaining ingredients.
2. Select sweet cycle on machine and press start.
3. Remove bread from pan while still warm. Allow to cool, then slice and serve.

# 6
# VEGETARIAN

Vegetable Pizza Calzones
Easy Italian Pasta Salad
Lemon-Pepper Pasta and Black Bean Salad
Simple Summer Salad
Terrific Tortellini Salad
Berry Delicious "Chicken" Salad
Surprising Taco Pizza
Simply Surprising Family-Sized Calzone
Smooth and Creamy Chili-Mac
Farm Vegetable Ragout in Crust
Creamy Coleslaw
Colorful Bean Salad
Classic Spinach Salad
Tomato and Spinach Salad
Full-Meal Salad
Cilantro Black Beans and Rice
Kid-Pleasing Tomato Cups
Chili con Corny

Whether you're a full-fledged vegetarian, or you're just trying to eat healthier, today's grocery products help to make meatless eating more delicious and enjoyable. Some of the recipes in this chapter may be familiar to you, and others may surprise you; but all require a minimum of ingredients, preparation, cooking, and clean-up time.

Many busy cooks rely heavily on make-ahead meals, so you'll find several recipes for days when time is at a premium. You'll also find several recipes that utilize partially prepared or frozen meat substitutes . . . and if you don't tell your family, they'll probably never notice. When a festive dinner is in order, try a few of the gourmet-style recipes (they're easier than you think to whip up). And for those households—like mine—where beans aren't a popular entrée, you'll discover spruced-up recipes that your kids will eat.

# Vegetable Pizza Calzones

*These rolled-up-pizzas have been a hit with dozens of folks, and are sure to bring compliments to the chef.*

Estimated preparation time: 10 minutes
Estimated baking time: 9 to 13 minutes
Makes 6 calzones

1. Preheat the oven to 425 degrees.
2. Lightly coat cookie sheet with cooking oil spray. Unroll pizza dough onto cookie sheet, and cut into six equal rectangles.
3. Place tomatoes, onions, peppers, and cheese in large bowl and mix to combine.
4. Divide vegetable and cheese mixture into six even portions. Put one portions on each rectangle and spread slightly. Starting at the longest side of each rectangle, fold dough over and fold to form a turnover-shaped packet. Pinch to seal edges. When done, they should resemble the commercial "hot pockets."
5. Bake for 9 to 13 minutes, or until tops of calzones are golden brown.

cooking oil spray
1 can (10 ounces) refrigerated pizza crust dough
1 can (15 ounce) diced tomatoes, drained
$\frac{1}{3}$ cup chopped onions (fresh or frozen)
$\frac{1}{3}$ cup diced green peppers (fresh or frozen)
1 $\frac{1}{4}$ cups shredded Italian-seasoned mozzarella cheese

# Easy Italian Pasta Salad

1 package (12 ounces) roasted garlic and red bell pepper rotelle pasta
3 cups chopped fresh broccoli
4 large carrots, thinly sliced
1 can (19 ounces) chick-peas, drained and rinsed
1 cup fat-free Italian salad dressing
¼ cup fat-free grated Parmesan cheese (optional)

*You can use this salad as a hearty main dish, or a savory side dish at potluck dinners and picnics.*

Estimated preparation time: 10 minutes
Estimated cooking time: 8 minutes
Estimated refrigeration time: 20 minutes
Makes 8 servings

1. Bring a large pot of water to a rolling boil. Add pasta, reduce heat to medium, and simmer, stirring occasionally, until pasta is tender. Drain and rinse with cold water.
2. Place cooked pasta, broccoli, carrots, and chick-peas in large bowl, and toss lightly. Drizzle salad dressing over pasta and vegetables and toss again.
3. Cover salad with plastic wrap and refrigerate for at least 20 minutes. Sprinkle with Parmesan cheese before serving, if desired.

# Lemon-Pepper Pasta and Black Bean Salad

*This winning pasta salad was the result of grabbing a handful of items from the pantry and improvising— it's best chilled, but can be served warm.*

Estimated preparation time: 10 minutes
Estimated cooking time: 8 minutes
Estimated refrigeration time: 20 minutes
Makes 8 servings

1 package (12 ounces) lemon-pepper penne rigate pasta
1 can (16 ounces) black beans, drained and rinsed
1 medium tomato, diced
1 cup frozen peas, thawed
¼ cup freshly squeezed or bottled lemon juice
¼ cup honey

1. Bring a large pot of water to a rolling boil. Add pasta, reduce heat to medium, and simmer, stirring occasionally, until pasta is tender. Drain and rinse with cold water.
2. Place cooked pasta, black beans, tomato, and peas in large bowl, and toss gently.
3. Place lemon juice and honey in small bowl and stir until honey has dissolved. Drizzle lemon and honey mixture over pasta and vegetables, then toss to coat.
4. Cover salad with plastic wrap and refrigerate for at least 20 minutes before serving.

# Simple Summer Salad

1 package (12 ounces) elbow
macaroni, uncooked
1 can (15 ounces) whole-
kernel corn, drained
and rinsed
2 cups diced zucchini
1 cup chopped dried apricots
2 tablespoons diced green
onion
¾ cup fat-free honey-mustard
salad dressing
2 honeydew melons,
quartered, seeds
scooped out (optional)

*For steamy evenings when it's just too hot to cook, toss this salad together and serve with fresh bread or rolls.*

Estimated preparation time: 10 minutes
Estimated cooking time: 8 minutes
Estimated refrigeration time: 20 minutes
Makes 8 servings

1. Bring a large pot of water to a rolling boil. Add pasta, reduce heat to medium, and simmer, stirring occasionally, until pasta is tender. Drain and rinse with cold water.
2. Place cooked pasta, corn, zucchini, apricots, and onion in large bowl, and toss gently. Drizzle salad dressing over pasta, vegetables, and fruit, and toss again.
3. Cover salad with plastic wrap and refrigerate for at least 20 minutes. Serve in quartered honeydew melons, if desired.

# Terrific Tortellini Salad

*Young children especially love this tasty treat, and it's satisfying enough to handle big appetites.*

Estimated preparation time: 5 minutes
Estimated cooking time: 10 minutes
Makes 6 servings

1. Bring a large pot of water to a rolling boil. Add tortellini, reduce heat to medium, and simmer, stirring occasionally, until pasta is tender. Add asparagus pieces during last 2 minutes of cooking. Drain and rinse with cold water.
2. Place tortellini and asparagus in large bowl, add tomato and basil, and toss gently. Drizzle pasta and vegetables with salad dressing, and toss again. Serve immediately.

2 packages (9 ounces each) refrigerated cheese-filled tortellini
1 pound asparagus, sliced into 1-inch inch pieces
1 pound cherry tomatoes, halved
2 tablespoons chopped fresh basil
⅔ cup fat-free Caesar salad dressing

# Berry Delicious "Chicken" Salad

1 can (16 ounces) diced
 peaches in juice,
 drained, juice reserved
2 tablespoons rice vinegar
1 tablespoon honey
1 package (16 ounces) salad
 greens
2 cups canned imitation diced
 chicken ("vegetable
 protein," available in
 the health food section
 of most grocery stores)
2 cups fresh raspberries
½ cup sliced celery

*Although no animal meat is used in this recipe, your family (or guests) will never know, and the sweet, tangy dressing makes the salad special.*

Estimated preparation time: 10 minutes
Makes 6 to 8 servings

1. Put reserved juice from peaches in small bowl, add rice vinegar and honey, and stir until dissolved.
2. Place salad greens, peaches, imitation chicken, raspberries, and celery in large bowl, and toss gently. Drizzle dressing over salad, and toss again.
3. Serve immediately, or refrigerate until ready to serve.

# Surprising Taco Pizza

*My guys love this pizza, and it's far healthier than anything that can be delivered. Better yet, it's ready in a flash!*

Estimated preparation time: 3 minutes
Estimated baking time: 15 minutes
Makes 12 square slices of pizza

cooking oil spray
1 can (10 ounces) refrigerated pizza crust dough
½ cup picante sauce
1½ cups Harvest Burgers For Recipes (meat substitute)
1 cup shredded fat-free cheddar cheese

1. Preheat oven to 400 degrees.
2. Lightly coat a cookie sheet with cooking oil spray. Press canned pizza dough evenly onto the cookie sheet and spread picante sauce over dough. Sprinkle with meat substitute, then with cheese.
3. Bake for about 15 minutes, or until cheese begins to bubble.

# Simply Surprising Family-Sized Calzone

2 cups Harvest Burgers For Recipes (meat substitute)
1 cup shredded reduced-fat Italian cheese mixture
1 medium tomato, diced
2 green onions, finely diced
½ teaspoon Italian seasoning
½ teaspoon garlic powder
1 can (10 ounces) refrigerated pizza crust dough

*When your gang is gathered 'round the television watching the big game, pop this in the oven and prepare for enthusiastic praise!*

Estimated preparation time: 5 minutes
Estimated baking time: 20 minutes
Makes 6 servings

1. Preheat oven to 400 degrees.
2. Place meat substitute, shredded cheese, tomato, and green onions in medium mixing bowl. Add Italian seasoning and garlic powder and toss lightly to mix.
3. Unroll pizza crust dough on a clean, flat surface. Spoon filling into the center of the dough (lengthwise). Carefully pull up the sides of the dough and pinch together in a seam down the center; roll and pinch ends to seal.
4. Bake for about 20 minutes, or until golden brown. Allow to cool slightly before slicing and serving.

# Smooth and Creamy Chili-Mac

*If hearty appetites demand a hot, filling meal, serve up this chili with rolls or cornbread.*

Estimated preparation time: 3 minutes
Estimated cooking time: 12 minutes
Makes 8 hearty servings

1. Place all ingredients except sour cream in medium nonstick pot. Heat over medium-low heat until mixture begins to bubble, stirring occasionally.
2. Reduce heat to low, cover, and continue cooking for 5 to 7 minutes, or until macaroni is cooked thoroughly.
3. Serve in individual bowls. Top with a dollop of nonfat sour cream if desired.

1 can (15 ounces) diced tomatoes
1 can (10 ounces) tomato soup
1½ cups water
1 can (16 ounces) red kidney beans, drained and rinsed
1 box (7.25 ounces) macaroni and cheese
½ teaspoon chili powder
nonfat sour cream (optional)

# Farm Vegetable Ragout in Crust

1 package (16 ounces) frozen
    Midwest-style
    vegetables (broccoli,
    carrots, cauliflower,
    peas), thawed
1 can (16 ounces) red kidney
    beans, drained and
    rinsed
1 medium tomato, diced
$\frac{1}{4}$ cup reduced-fat honey-
    mustard salad dressing
2 cans (8 ounces each)
    reduced-fat crescent
    roll dough

*Would you like a power-packed dinner with a zesty, sweet twist? This recipe will meet the challenge.*

Estimated preparation time: 10 minutes
Estimated baking time: 8 minutes
Makes 4 generous servings

1. Preheat oven to 375 degrees.
2. Combine vegetables, beans, and diced tomato in medium mixing bowl. Drizzle salad dressing over mixture and toss lightly.
3. Spoon seasoned vegetable mixture into 4 small ($1\frac{3}{4}$-cups) casserole dishes or ovenproof bowls.
4. Divide crescent roll dough into 4 rectangles, carefully pressing perforations together to seal. Using a pizza cutter or knife, slice each rectangle into 6 strips (lengthwise). Assemble the strips in a lattice pattern over each casserole, pressing ends to seal.
5. Bake for 8 minutes, or until golden brown.

# Creamy Coleslaw

*I've made many gallons of coleslaw over the past twenty years, and this is the indisputable favorite.*

Estimated preparation time: 5 minutes
Makes 6 servings

1. Place mayonnaise, lemon juice, vinegar, sugar, and flax seeds in large bowl and whisk together.
2. Add coleslaw mix and watercress, and toss gently to coat.

2 tablespoons mayonnaise
2 tablespoons lemon juice
2 tablespoons white balsamic vinegar or white vinegar
1 tablespoon sugar
2 teaspoons flax seeds (available at health food stores)
1 package (16 ounces) coleslaw mix
½ bunch watercress (about ¼ pound)

# Colorful Bean Salad

1 package (10 ounces) frozen green beans, thawed
1 can (16 ounces) white kidney beans, drained and rinsed
1 can (16 ounces) red kidney beans, drained and rinsed
1 red onion, chopped
½ cup fat-free Italian dressing
¼ cup chopped fresh cilantro
large lettuce leaves (optional)

*Three-bean salad has always been a staple dish during summertime picnics, but you can serve this adaptation any time of year.*

Estimated preparation time: 5 minutes
Makes 4 servings

1. Combine all ingredients except lettuce in large bowl, tossing to mix well.
2. If desired, use a large lettuce leaf as a serving bowl.

# Classic Spinach Salad

*Some classic recipes are hard to improve on. This salad is lower in fat—and it's meatless—but it's just as tasty as the original version.*

Estimated preparation time: 5 minutes
Makes 4 servings

1. Place spinach, mushrooms, tomatoes, and bacon bits in medium-sized bowl and toss to combine.
2. Combine vinegar, water, oil, and brown sugar in small glass bowl or large glass measuring cup. Whisk until well combined.
3. Drizzle dressing over salad and toss gently. Serve immediately.

2 cups chopped fresh spinach leaves
1 cup sliced mushrooms
1 pint cherry tomatoes, quartered
2 tablespoons imitation bacon bits
2 tablespoons cider vinegar
$\frac{1}{4}$ cup water
$\frac{1}{4}$ cup canola oil
1 tablespoon light brown sugar

# Tomato and Spinach Salad

¼ cup spicy tomato juice
2 teaspoons lemon juice
2 tablespoons vegetable oil
2 teaspoons minced fresh
    thyme
⅛ teaspoon salt
⅛ teaspoon coarsely ground
    pepper or cracked
    black pepper
⅛ teaspoon ground cumin
1 bag (10 ounces) fresh
    spinach
1 small red onion, finely sliced
1 pint cherry tomatoes,
    quartered

*Here's a spicy, robust salad that becomes a meal in a bowl when served with fresh bread or rolls.*

Estimated preparation time: 5 minutes
Makes 4 servings

1. Whisk together juices, oil, and spices in large bowl.
2. Add remaining ingredients and toss to coat evenly.

# Full-Meal Salad

*When you're feeding a crowd, this salad will provide ample servings. Add a decorative platter of wheat crackers, and enjoy the satisfied smiles after dinner.*

Estimated preparation time: 15 minutes
Makes 8 servings

1. Layer lettuce, tomatoes, mushrooms, peas, cheese, and onions in large serving bowl.
2. Spread salad dressing over onions to edge of bowl, then cover. Refrigerate several hours or overnight. Garnish with chives and parsley.

6 cups shredded iceberg lettuce
2 cups chopped tomatoes
2 cups sliced mushrooms
1 package (10 ounces) frozen peas, thawed and drained
4 ounces fat-free cheddar cheese, cubed
½ medium red onion, sliced into rings (about 1 cup rings)
2 cups light salad dressing
1 tablespoon chopped chives, for garnish
1 small bunch fresh parsley sprigs, for garnish

# Cilantro Black Beans and Rice

1 can (13¼ ounces) vegetable
  broth
½ cup raw white rice
1 can (16 ounces) black
  beans, drained and
  rinsed
½ teaspoon grated lemon peel
½ cup loosely packed cilantro
  leaves

*Simple and mild, this dish is ideal for kids who turn their noses up at spicier southwestern fare.*

Estimated preparation time: 5 minutes
Estimated cooking time: 15 minutes
Makes 4 servings

1. Bring broth to a boil in medium saucepan. Add rice and reduce heat to low. Cover and let simmer for 15 minutes.
2. Stir in black beans and lemon peel, and continue cooking until rice is tender and liquid is completely absorbed (about 5 minutes).
3. Top with cilantro leaves and serve.

# Kid-Pleasing Tomato Cups

*Kids will have fun assembling—and eating—these colorful treats.*

Estimated preparation time: 10 minutes
Makes 6 servings

1. Place quinoa, peas, parsley, onion, oil, and orange peel in medium bowl, and toss to combine well. Season to taste with salt and pepper.
2. Fill tomatoes with quinoa mixture and serve.

2 cups cooked quinoa
1 cup frozen green peas, thawed
¼ cup chopped fresh parsley
½ small red onion, minced
1 teaspoon canola oil
1 teaspoon grated orange peel
salt and pepper
6 tomatoes, hollowed out

# Chili con Corny

1 can (15 ounces) diced
    tomatoes
1 can (16 ounces) hot chili
    beans
1 can (16 ounces) black
    beans, drained
1 can (15 ounces) whole-
    kernel corn
1 cup water

*Who'd think that pouring four cans of vegetables and beans into a pot could bring about such an appealing bowl of chili? You will when you assemble this recipe in five easy minutes.*

Estimated preparation time: 5 minutes
Estimated cooking time: 10 to 12 minutes
Makes 6 to 8 servings

1. Place all ingredients in medium nonstick pot and stir. Bring to a low boil over medium-low heat, stirring occasionally, until hot, about 10 minutes.
2. Remove from heat and serve.

# 7
# SIDE DISHES

Saucy Green Beans
Sweetly Seasoned Beets
Bay-Watcher Carrots
Creamy Herbed Corn
Two Peas and Dill Surprise
Simple Spinach and Broccoli
Last-Minute Salad
Fast Herbed Salad
Fast Oriental-Style Salad
Red, White, and Greens
    Salad

Side-Dish Fettuccini
Creamy Shells and Cheese
Lemon-Dill Tortellini
Speedy Almond Rice
Brown Rice Pilaf
Cheesy Mashed Potatoes
Beefy Mashed Potatoes
Fast Potato Pancakes
Easy Au Gratin Potatoes
Low-Sugar Sweet Potatoes

Pulling the main dish together for dinner can be challenging enough—why tackle complicated side dishes? You'll be amazed at how fast, easy, and delicious the following recipes are. The secret lies on grocery store shelves. Did you know that canned vegetables are no less nutritious than frozen ones, or that quick-cooking rice and pasta can be spruced up and ready to serve in the time it takes to set the table?

You'll enjoy recipes that are as basic as opening a few cans and adding a pinch of seasoning. You'll have winning salads in a snap using packaged salad greens and a few other ingredients. Rice and pasta dishes get rave reviews with a few easy, extra touches; and if you think potatoes are boring, you're in for a big surprise! Keep your pantry and freezer stocked with a few basics (listed in chapter 1), and side dishes are simple to whip up.

# Saucy Green Beans

*My youngest is a green-vegetable phobe, but he loves this dish (and sometimes asks for seconds).*

Estimated preparation time: 5 minutes
Estimated cooking time: 12 minutes
Makes 6 servings

1 tablespoon light canola oil
½ cup chopped onion
2 cans (14.5 ounces each) French-style green beans
3 tablespoons white vinegar
1 beef bouillon cube
2 tablespoons cornstarch

1. Preheat medium nonstick pot over medium-high heat. Add oil and onion, and stir. Pour green beans and their liquid into pot, and add vinegar and bouillon cube.
2. Cook until bouillon cube has dissolved. Reduce heat to low and stir in cornstarch. Continue stirring constantly until sauce thickens.
3. Remove from heat and serve.

# Sweetly Seasoned Beets

1 can (16 ounces) sliced beets,
  drained
¼ cup orange juice
½ teaspoon chopped fresh
  savory
½ teaspoon chopped fresh
  basil

*These are not bland, salad bar–style beets. Once your family has tried them, they'll become a healthy favorite.*

Estimated preparation time: 5 minutes
Estimated cooking time: 10 minutes
Makes 4 servings

1. Place all ingredients in small nonstick pot. Cook over medium heat until liquid begins to boil.
2. Reduce heat to low and simmer, uncovered, for 5 minutes, stirring occasionally.

# Bay-Watcher Carrots

*If you're used to serving carrots seasoned with margarine, this recipe packs more flavor into every vitamin-filled bite . . . and it's much lower in fat!*

1 can (15 ounces) sliced
    carrots
1 green onion, finely diced
1 beef bouillon cube
1 bay leaf

Estimated preparation time: 5 minutes
Estimated cooking time: 10 minutes
Makes 4 servings

1. Pour canned carrots and their liquid into small non-stick pot. Add remaining ingredients.
2. Cook over medium heat, stirring occasionally, until bouillon has dissolved.
3. Reduce heat to low and simmer, uncovered, for 5 minutes.

# Creamy Herbed Corn

1 can (15 ounces) whole-
    kernel golden corn
1 can (15 ounces) whole-
    kernel white corn
1 can (10.75 ounces) reduced-
    fat condensed cream of
    celery soup
½ teaspoon celery seed
1 tablespoon chopped chives

*Here's a new twist on an old favorite: If you have leftovers from this recipe, puree in a blender and stir into a purchased corn muffin mix (in place of liquid)*

Estimated preparation time: 5 minutes
Estimated cooking time: 7 minutes
Makes 8 servings

1. Pour corn and its liquid into medium nonstick pot. Add soup, celery seed, and chives.
2. Cook over medium-low heat, stirring occasionally, until sauce is smooth and begins to bubble.

# Two Peas and Dill Surprise

*A colorful dish with a lot of flavor, this is almost a meal in itself. Enjoy it as a side dish; the next night, heat up a can of your favorite creamed soup, stir in the leftovers, and pour it over pasta for a quick dinner (angel hair pasta works very well).*

1 can (15 ounces) tender
   sweet peas, drained
1 can (16 ounces) chick-peas,
   drained
1 tablespoon light olive oil
1 tablespoon chopped fresh
   dill

Estimated preparation time: 3 minutes
Estimated cooking time: 4 to 5 minutes
Makes 8 servings

1. Place all ingredients in microwavable casserole dish, toss gently, and cover.
2. Microwave on high for 4 to 5 minutes, or until the peas are heated thoroughly.

# Simple Spinach and Broccoli

1 can (15 ounces) chopped
   spinach, drained
1 cup cooked broccoli (from
   leftovers)
1 tablespoon reduced-fat
   margarine
1 tablespoon lemon juice
$\frac{1}{4}$ teaspoon coarsely ground
   pepper

*In the mood for a quick, crustless pie? This dish is fabulous on its own, but you can stir leftovers into a batter made of 1 cup biscuit mix, 4 eggs, $\frac{1}{2}$ cup nonfat sour cream, and $\frac{1}{2}$ cup nonfat milk. Then pour it into a pie pan and bake at 375 degrees for 20 minutes.*

Estimated preparation time: 3 minutes
Estimated cooking time: 4 to 5 minutes
Makes 6 servings

1. Place all ingredients in microwavable casserole dish, stir, and cover.
2. Microwave on high for 4 to 5 minutes, or until vegetables are heated thoroughly.

# Last-Minute Salad

*You're running late, you've grabbed a deli-roasted chicken on your way home, and you'd like a little something extra with your meal; this recipe couldn't be simpler.*

1 package (16 ounces) salad
    greens
1 cup sliced fresh mushrooms
10 to 12 cherry tomatoes
2 tablespoons roasted shelled
    sunflower seeds or
    nuts

Estimated preparation time: 3 minutes
Makes 6 servings

1. Place salad greens in medium bowl, arrange mushrooms and tomatoes on top, and sprinkle with seeds or nuts.
2. Serve with your favorite dressings, or olive oil and vinegar.

. . . . . . . . . . . . . . . . .

Note: Add drained, water-packed tuna to any remaining salad for a quick, low-fat lunch.

. . . . . . . . . . . . . . . . .

# Fast Herbed Salad

1 package (16 ounces) salad greens
1 small bunch lemon basil or sweet basil
2 tablespoons chopped fresh thyme
¼ cup fat-free Italian dressing

*For a special gourmet touch to an everyday salad, add fresh herbs and take a bow.*

Estimated preparation time: 5 minutes
Makes 6 servings

1. Place salad greens and herbs in medium bowl.
2. Drizzle with dressing and toss lightly.

Note: Add diced cooked beef and 1 tablespoon Parmesan cheese to any remaining salad for a quick lunch.

# Fast Oriental-Style Salad

*Children of all ages love this colorful, crunchy, and zesty salad—and it's ready in minutes!*

Estimated preparation time: 5 minutes
Makes 8 servings

1. Place salad greens and mixed vegetables in medium bowl and toss.
2. Sprinkle with noodles and drizzle with dressing.

................

Note: Add diced cooked chicken to any remaining salad for a quick lunch.

................

1 package (16 ounces) salad greens
2 cups frozen Oriental-style vegetables, thawed and drained
¼ cup chow mein noodles (such as Chun King brand)
½ cup sweet and spicy type dressing (such as Kraft brand Catalina)

# Red, White, and Greens Salad

1 package (16 ounces) salad
    greens
1 cup frozen broccoli and
    cauliflower mixture,
    thawed and drained
10 cherry tomatoes, halved
⅓ cup fat-free ranch dressing

*Cool, creamy, and eye-appealing, this salad will wow your guests or potluck gang—and they'll never know you made is so quickly.*

Estimated preparation time: 7 minutes
Makes 6 servings

1. Place salad greens in medium bowl.
2. Arrange other vegetables on top and drizzle with dressing.

# Side-Dish Fettuccini

*This side dish can also be served as a main dish on a hectic night (serve beans, nuts, or dairy products for protein). The fresh herbs add zing to many convenience foods. Try experimenting with different flavor combinations!*

Estimated preparation time: 7 minutes
Estimated cooking time: 20 minutes conventional,
   8 minutes microwave
Makes 4 servings

1 package (5.1 ounces) fettuccini Alfredo noodle mix
1 tablespoon chopped fresh basil
1 tablespoon chopped fresh oregano
¼ teaspoon garlic powder
⅓ cup plain dried bread crumbs

1. Prepare pasta according to package instructions.
2. Add basil, oregano, and garlic powder and toss to combine. Sprinkle with bread crumbs and serve.

# Creamy Shells and Cheese

1 package (5.1 ounces) shells
    and cheese noodle mix
    (such as Noodle-Roni
    brand)
$\frac{1}{2}$ cup nonfat sour cream
1 teaspoon chopped chives

*Tired of plain old macaroni and cheese? You and your family will love this easy, creamy recipe!*

Estimated preparation time: 7 minutes
Estimated cooking time: 20 minutes conventional,
    8 minutes microwave
Makes 4 servings

1. Prepare pasta according to package instructions.
2. Stir in sour cream, sprinkle with chives, and serve.

# Lemon-Dill Tortellini

*This surprising combination is delicious. If you have leftover Lemon-Dill Tortellini, toss it with 1 cup of salad greens for a quick lunch.*

1 package (9 ounces) fresh cheese tortellini
1 tablespoon margarine, melted
1 tablespoon lemon juice
2 teaspoons chopped fresh dill

Estimated preparation time: 7 minutes
Estimated cooking time: 8 to 10 minutes
Makes 6 servings

1. Prepare pasta according to package directions.
2. Whisk margarine, lemon juice, and dill in small bowl.
3. Pour sauce over pasta, toss to combine, and serve.

# Speedy Almond Rice

½ cup slivered almonds
2 tablespoons reduced-fat
 margarine
1 cup water
1 cup instant rice (such as
 Minute Rice brand)
¼ teaspoon cinnamon

*When you don't have time to steam traditional rice, instant versions work well, but may need a little help in the flavor department; this recipe is one solution.*

Estimated preparation time: 3 minutes
Estimated cooking time: 5 minutes
Makes 4 servings

1. Place all ingredients in microwavable casserole dish, cover, and microwave on high for 3 minutes. Stir.
2. Microwave uncovered for an additional 2 minutes, and stir again.

# Brown Rice Pilaf

*A big hit with the kids, this side dish works well with just about any beef, pork, or poultry.*

Estimated preparation time: 7 minutes
Estimated cooking time: 7 to 8 minutes
Makes 4 servings

1. Pour broth and water into medium nonstick pot and bring to boil over medium heat.
2. Stir in rice, reduce temperature to low, and simmer for 2 minutes. Remove from heat.
3. Stir in onion and raisins. Cover and let sit 2 to 3 minutes.

· · · · · · · · · · · · · · · ·

Note: Sprinkle Brown Rice Pilaf with $\frac{1}{8}$ teaspoon saffron and $\frac{1}{8}$ teaspoon ginger for a Middle Eastern flavor.

· · · · · · · · · · · · · · · ·

1 can (10.75 ounces) chicken broth
$\frac{1}{3}$ cup water
2 cups instant brown rice (such as Uncle Ben's brand)
1 green onion, finely chopped
$\frac{1}{2}$ cup raisins

# Cheesy Mashed Potatoes

1⅓ cups water
½ cup nonfat milk
1⅓ cups instant mashed
    potato flakes
¼ teaspoon coarsely ground
    pepper
¼ teaspoon paprika
½ cup reduced-fat shredded
    cheddar cheese

*Children can't seem to get enough of this alternative "comfort food."*

Estimated preparation time: 5 minutes
Estimated cooking time: 3 minutes
Makes 4 servings

1. Pour water and milk into microwavable casserole dish, add potato flakes, and stir.
2. Microwave on high, uncovered, for 3 minutes.
3. Sprinkle with pepper, paprika, and cheese, stirring until smooth.

# Beefy Mashed Potatoes

*Much more flavorful than ordinary mashed potatoes, this dish is a treat. Because there are no dairy products in this recipe, it's perfect for lactose-intolerant family members.*

1 can (10 ounces) beef broth
½ cup water
1⅓ cups instant mashed
  potato flakes
¼ teaspoon coarsely ground
  pepper

Estimated preparation time: 5 minutes
Estimated cooking time: 3 minutes
Makes 4 servings

1. Pour broth and water into microwavable casserole dish. Stir in potato flakes and pepper.
2. Microwave on high for 3 minutes, stir, and serve.

# Fast Potato Pancakes

2 cups frozen mashed
    potatoes, thawed
¼ cup flour
1 egg
1 cup nonfat sour cream
¼ cup chopped fresh chives
cooking oil spray

*With my Germanic background, I've enjoyed potato pancakes all of my life; but these days I need a streamlined, lower-fat recipe. This is it.*

Estimated preparation time: 7 minutes
Estimated cooking time: 10 to 12 minutes total
Makes 12 small pancakes, or 4 servings

1. Preheat large nonstick skillet or griddle over medium heat.
2. Place mashed potatoes, flour, egg, sour cream, and chives in medium bowl and mix until well combined. Batter will be thick.
3. Lightly coat hot skillet with cooking oil spray. Drop batter onto surface using ¼ cup measure. Cook 2 to 3 minutes on each side.

# Easy Au Gratin Potatoes

*Rich and creamy—yet lower in fat than boxed varieties—these potatoes will satisfy hearty appetites.*

Estimated preparation time: 7 minutes
Estimated cooking time: 14 minutes
Makes 4 servings

1. Lightly coat microwavable casserole dish with cooking oil spray.
2. Place onions in bottom of dish and microwave on high for 1 minute.
3. Add undiluted soup and cream cheese, then microwave on high for 3 minutes.
4. Stir in hash browns, cover, and microwave on high for an additional 10 minutes.

. . . . . . . . . . . . . . . .

Note: Try this recipe using frozen cottage-style fries for a different look. Be sure to increase the final cooking time to 12 minutes.

. . . . . . . . . . . . . . . .

cooking oil spray
½ cup chopped onion (fresh or frozen )
1 can (10.75 ounces) reduced-fat condensed cream of mushroom soup
2 ounces reduced-fat cream cheese, cubed
3 cups frozen hash browns

# Low-Sugar Sweet Potatoes

1 can (16 ounces) sweet
   potatoes, drained and
   diced
1 can (16 ounces) crushed
   pineapple, drained
2 tablespoons reduced-fat
   margarine, cut into
   small pats
2 teaspoons sugar substitute
   for baking (such as
   Equal or Measure
   brands)

*Almost everyone loves candied yams, but if you'd like a lower-sugar version that's just as tasty, try these. You can double or triple this recipe for holiday entertaining.*

Estimated preparation time: 10 minutes
Estimated cooking time: 5 minutes
Makes 4 servings

1. Combine sweet potatoes and pineapple in microwavable casserole dish. Top with margarine and sugar substitute.
2. Cover, and microwave on high for 5 minutes.

# 8
# BAKING

Basic Biscuit Mix
Easy Country-Style Biscuits
Easy Cheese Biscuits
Easy Herbed Biscuits
Milk-Free Biscuit Mix
Dairy-Less Dinner Biscuits
Basic Muffin Mix
Yummy Blueberry Muffins
Protein-Packed Cranberry
  Muffins
Marvelous Mixed-Fruit
  Muffins
Almost-Homemade Apple
  Pie
Almost-Homemade Blue-
  berry Pie
Almost-Homemade
  Cherry Pie

Quick and Easy Strudel
Angel-Custard Cake
Simply Banana-Nut
  Cookie Bars
Basic Sugar Cookies
Low-Fat Chocolate Chewy
  Cookie Bars
Easiest Boston Cream Pie
Heavenly Chocolate
  Cherry Cake
Sinfully Low-Fat Choco-
  late Cheesecake
Fast and Low-Fat Pump-
  kin Pie
Easiest Apple "Crisp" Pie
Fruit and Easy Mousse

My mother and grandmother baked almost daily, and the heavenly aroma of fresh-from-the-oven treats filled their homes with love. As a new mother, I tried to live up to the examples I'd had, but soon found that the heirloom recipes were both time consuming and quite fattening. A few years ago I began developing fast, low-fat alternatives for many of my childhood favorites.

There are certainly many varieties of refrigerated or frozen products on the market, and packaged mixes in regular and reduced-fat styles; the cost of those products can be a bit steep sometimes, and "homemade" is a better budget alternative when possible. In this chapter, you'll find basic mix recipes for biscuits and muffins, with variations for each. You'll also find recipes for power baking on the weekend, quicker, healthier cookies, and no-bake miracles that get rave reviews.

# Basic Biscuit Mix

*This Basic Biscuit Mix is easy to prepare, stays fresh for weeks, and replaces commercial (boxed) mixes— it's also lower in fat and calories.*

6 cups bread flour
1 cup dry buttermilk (available
    in the baking section
    of your grocery store)
1 ½ teaspoons iodized salt
¼ cup baking powder
½ cup reduced-fat margarine,
    softened

Estimated preparation time: about 5 minutes
Makes about 8 cups biscuit mix

1. Place all ingredients in food processor and pulse until well combined.
2. Store mix in airtight container and refrigerate for up to 4 weeks.

# Easy Country-Style Biscuits

2 cups Basic Biscuit Mix (page 147)
1 teaspoon sugar
⅔ cup water

*Here's the perfect, last-minute mealtime batch of biscuits.*

Estimated preparation time: 10 minutes
Estimated baking time: 8 to 10 minutes
Makes 12 biscuits

1. Preheat oven to 425 degrees.
2. Place all ingredients in medium bowl and stir with fork to combine.
3. Turn dough onto floured surface and knead for 2 minutes; allow to rest for 2 minutes.
4. Roll out dough ¼ inch thick and cut into rounds using cookie cutter or glass dipped in flour.
5. Arrange biscuits on nonstick cookie sheet and bake for 8 to 10 minutes.

# Easy Cheese Biscuits

*Great with soups, chili, or meal-sized salads, these biscuits will be gobbled up quickly.*

2 cups Basic Biscuit Mix (page 147)
$\frac{1}{4}$ cup reduced-fat Parmesan cheese
$\frac{2}{3}$ cup water

Estimated preparation time: 10 minutes
Estimated baking time: 8 to 10 minutes
Makes 12 biscuits

1. Preheat oven to 425 degrees.
2. Place all ingredients in medium bowl and stir with fork to combine.
3. Turn dough onto floured surface and knead for 2 minutes; allow to rest for 2 minutes.
4. Roll out dough $\frac{1}{4}$ inch thick and cut into rounds using cookie cutter or glass dipped in flour.
5. Arrange biscuits on nonstick cookie sheet and bake for 8 to 10 minutes.

# Easy Herbed Biscuits

2 cups Basic Biscuit Mix (page 147)
¼ teaspoon sage
½ teaspoon thyme
⅔ cups water

*Use fresh herbs and fresh herb blends for wonderfully aromatic biscuits.*

Estimated preparation time: 10 minutes
Estimated baking time: 8 to 10 minutes
Makes 12 biscuits

1. Preheat oven to 425 degrees.
2. Place all ingredients in medium bowl and stir with fork to combine.
3. Turn dough onto floured surface and knead for 2 minutes; allow to rest for 2 minutes.
4. Roll out dough ¼ inch thick and cut into rounds using cookie cutter or glass dipped in flour.
5. Arrange biscuits on nonstick cookie sheet and bake for 8 to 10 minutes.

# Milk-Free Biscuit Mix

*Many families today grapple with allergies and follow restricted diets. This recipe is ideal for lactose-intolerant family members, but the taste is not identical to that of traditional biscuits.*

6 cups bread flour
1 cup powdered low-iron soy formula (available near baby food)
1½ teaspoons iodized salt
¼ cup plus 1 teaspoon baking powder
½ cup reduced-fat dairy-free margarine, softened

Estimated preparation time: about 5 minutes
Makes about 8 cups mix

1. Place all ingredients in food processor and pulse until well combined.
2. Store mix in an airtight container and refrigerate for up to 4 weeks.

# Dairy-Less Dinner Biscuits

2 cups Milk-Free Biscuit Mix
(page 151)
1 teaspoon sugar
⅛ teaspoon cumin
⅔ cup water

*Although tasty on their own, you can add fresh herbs or herb blends to add zest to these easy biscuits.*

Estimated preparation time: 10 minutes
Estimated baking time: 8 to 10 minutes
Makes 12 biscuits

1. Preheat oven to 425 degrees.
2. Place all ingredients in medium bowl and stir with fork to combine.
3. Turn dough onto floured surface and knead for 2 minutes; allow to rest for 2 minutes.
4. Roll out dough ¼ inch thick and cut into rounds using cookie cutter or glass dipped in flour.
5. Arrange biscuits on nonstick cookie sheet and bake for 8 to 10 minutes.

# Basic Muffin Mix

*Muffins are a popular breakfast or after-school treat in our home, and with this mix, I'm always ready to whip up a quick batch. Substitute powdered low-iron soy formula for dry milk if dairy is a problem in your household.*

2 cups whole wheat flour
2 cups all-purpose flour
1 cup oat bran or wheat germ
2 cups nonfat dry milk
2 cups sugar
1 tablespoon plus 1 teaspoon
    baking powder
1 teaspoon baking soda
1 teaspoon salt

Estimated preparation time: 10 minutes
Makes about 9 cups mix

1. Mix all ingredients thoroughly in large bowl.
2. Store in airtight container in pantry or cupboard for up to 4 weeks, or in airtight freezer bags in the freezer for up to 4 months.

Baking      **153**

# Yummy Blueberry Muffins

cooking oil spray
2 cups Basic Muffin Mix
        (page 153)
1 egg
2 tablespoon canola oil
¾ cup water
½ cup orange juice
½ pint fresh blueberries (or
        frozen and thawed)

*Take advantage of seasonal specials; buy blueberries in large quantities in season, and store them in zip-top freezer bags for year 'round goodies.*

Estimated preparation time: 10 minutes
Estimated baking time: 15 minutes
Makes 12 muffins

1. Preheat oven to 400 degrees.
2. Lightly coat muffin tin with cooking oil spray.
3. Combine muffin mix, egg, oil, water, and orange juice in medium bowl until just moistened. Batter will be lumpy. Fold in blueberries.
4. Spoon batter into muffin tin and bake for 15 minutes.

Note: All baked muffins can be frozen in airtight freezer bags and microwaved for a quick breakfast or snack.

# Protein-Packed Cranberry Muffins

*These muffins are an ideal source of calcium, iron, and many vitamins—they're also delicious!*

Estimated preparation time: 10 minutes
Estimated baking time: 15 minutes
Makes 12 muffins

1. Preheat oven to 400 degrees.
2. Lightly coat muffin tin with cooking oil spray.
3. Combine muffin mix, egg, oil, milk, and yogurt in medium bowl until moistened. Batter will be lumpy. Fold in cranberries.
4. Spoon batter into muffin tin and bake for 15 minutes.

cooking oil spray
2 cups Basic Muffin Mix
(page 153)
1 egg
1 tablespoon canola oil
$\frac{2}{3}$ cup nonfat milk
1 cup nonfat plain yogurt or
sour cream
1½ cups dried cranberries

# Marvelous Mixed-Fruit Muffins

cooking oil spray
2 cups Basic Muffin Mix
      (page 153)
1 egg
1 tablespoon canola oil
¾ cup water
⅓ cup unsweetened
      applesauce
1 ripe banana, mashed
1 cup raisins

*Try these muffins with honey butter on a cold, dreary day, or as a breakfast surprise.*

Estimated preparation time: 10 minutes
Estimated baking time: 15 minutes
Makes 12 muffins

1. Preheat oven to 400 degrees.
2. Lightly coat muffin tin with cooking oil spray.
3. Combine muffin mix, egg, oil, water, applesauce, and banana in medium bowl until moistened. Batter will be lumpy. Fold in raisins.
4. Spoon batter into muffin tin and bake for 15 minutes.

# Almost-Homemade Apple Pie

*When I don't have time to bake a homemade pie from scratch—but I want my home to smell like I have—I jazz up purchased, frozen pies and enjoy the compliments.*

1 frozen apple pie (9 inches)
½ cup powdered sugar
½ teaspoon cinnamon
1 tablespoon water
¼ cup chopped nuts

Estimated preparation time: 10 minutes
Estimated baking time: varies according to brand of
    frozen pie
Makes 8 medium or 10 small servings

1. Bake frozen pie according to package directions. Cool.
2. Place powdered sugar, cinnamon, and water in small
   bowl and stir with fork until smooth.
3. Spread frosting over top of cooled pie, sprinkle with
   nuts, and serve.

# Almost-Homemade Blueberry Pie

1 frozen blueberry pie
    (9 inches)
½ cup powdered sugar
1 tablespoon plus ½ teaspoon
    lemon juice
1 teaspoon lemon zest

*Did your child volunteer you for the PTA bake sale? This last-minute solution will save your sanity and your pride.*

Estimated preparation time: 10 minutes
Estimated baking time: varies according to brand of
    frozen pie
Makes 8 medium servings or 10 small servings

1. Prepare pie according to package directions. Cool.
2. Place powdered sugar and lemon juice in small bowl and stir with fork until smooth. Frosting will be thin.
3. Spread frosting over cooled pie, sprinkle with lemon zest, and serve.

# Almost-Homemade Cherry Pie

*Make a few of these on (or near) President's Day, and give the extras to neighbors or coworkers.*

1 frozen cherry pie (9 inches)
½ cup cherry preserves
¼ cup chopped pecans

Estimated preparation time: 5 minutes
Estimated baking time: varies according to frozen pie
　brand
Makes 8 medium servings or 10 small servings

1. Prepare pie according to package directions. Cool.
2. Place preserves in small, microwavable bowl and microwave on high, uncovered, for 1 minute.
3. Stir and spread on cooled pie. Sprinkle with nuts and serve.

# Quick and Easy Strudel

1 package (15 ounces)
    refrigerated pie crusts
1 can (16 ounces) light apple
    pie filling
½ cup reduced-fat biscuit mix
    (or Basic Biscuit Mix,
    page 147)
1 tub (4 ounces) nonfat cream
    cheese spread
¼ cup powdered sugar
¼ cup chopped nuts

*My mother was mistress of strudels, and she received compliments for every one she baked—this recipe is my version. Before frosting, you can freeze one strudel in an airtight freezer bag for up to one month.*

Estimated preparation time: 15 minutes
Estimated baking time: 15 minutes
Makes 8 to 10 servings

1. Preheat oven to 400 degrees.
2. Bring pie crusts to room temperature and unfold on lightly floured surface.
3. Combine pie filling and biscuit mix in medium bowl.
4. Spoon half of mixture down the center of each pie crust. Carefully fold opposite sides of crusts toward center, overlapping about 1 inch to form semi-rectangular shape. Fold up remaining edges just to touch center seams.
5. Transfer pastries to nonstick cookie sheet and bake for 15 minutes, or until golden brown. Remove from oven, cool, and transfer to serving platters.
6. Place cream cheese spread and sugar in a small bowl and combine until well blended. Spread half the mixture onto each cooled pastry.
7. Sprinkle each strudel with 2 tablespoons nuts and serve.

· · · · · · · · · · · · · · · ·

Variations:

Cheery, Cherry Strudel: *Omit apple pie filling and substitute 1 can light cherry pie filling.*

Purely Peach Strudel: *Omit apple pie filling and substitute 1 can peach pie filling, or 3 cups sliced canned peaches, drained.*

Holiday Mincemeat Strudel: *Omit apple pie filling and substitute 2 cups reduced-fat mincemeat from jar. Omit cream cheese frosting and nuts, and substitute a sprinkling of lemon-flavored confectioner's sugar.*

· · · · · · · · · · · · · · · ·

# Angel-Custard Cake

cooking oil spray
1 ready-made angel food cake
 (10 to 12 ounces)
1 can (8 ounces) evaporated
 skim milk
2 cartons (4 ounces each) egg
 substitute, thawed, or
 4 eggs, beaten
2 tablespoons sugar
¼ teaspoon nutmeg
1 tub (8 ounces) nonfat non-
 dairy whipped topping,
 thawed (optional)
fresh fruit (optional)

*This is an adaptation of my grandmother's favorite dessert recipe.*

Estimated preparation time: 15 minutes
Estimated baking time: 15 minutes
Makes 12 servings

1. Preheat oven to 375 degrees.
2. Lightly coat $9 \times 13$-inch baking dish with cooking oil spray.
3. Cut angel food cake into bite-sized cubes and arrange in bottom of prepared baking dish, making sure that cake pieces are touching one another.
4. Place milk, egg substitute, sugar, and nutmeg in medium bowl and whisk together. Pour over cake pieces.
5. Cover baking dish with aluminum foil and bake for 15 minutes. Remove from oven, uncover, and cool. Serve with whipped topping or fresh fruit. Refrigerate leftover cake after serving, discarding any uneaten cake after 3 days.

# Simply Banana-Nut Cookie Bars

*This began as an accidental recipe, but received such rave reviews that it's been gobbled up dozens of times.*

Estimated preparation time: 5 minutes
Estimated baking time: 20 to 25 minutes
Makes 1 dozen bar cookies

¼ cup reduced-fat margarine,
    softened
¾ cup sugar
1 egg
2 cups reduced-fat biscuit mix
2 ripe bananas, mashed
½ cup chopped nuts
cooking oil spray

1. Preheat oven to 350 degrees.
2. Cream together margarine, sugar, and egg in medium bowl. Slowly stir in biscuit mix. Batter will be stiff. Fold in mashed bananas and chopped nuts.
3. Lightly coat $9 \times 9$-inch nonstick baking dish with cooking oil spray. Spread batter in dish.
4. Bake for 20 to 25 minutes, or until golden brown. Remove from oven, cool, and slice into bars.

# Basic Sugar Cookies

2 cups reduced-fat biscuit mix
$\frac{2}{3}$ cup sugar
$\frac{1}{2}$ cup reduced-fat margarine,
    softened
1 egg
$\frac{1}{3}$ cup nonfat milk
1 teaspoon vanilla

*I keep plenty of this mix on hand whenever possible, because it's common for my sons to announce before bedtime that I'm to bake cookies for a class party the next day.*

Estimated preparation time: 3 minutes
Estimated baking time: 8 to 10 minutes
Makes 3 dozen cookies

1. Preheat oven to 350 degrees.
2. Place biscuit mix and sugar in medium bowl and cut in softened margarine. Add remaining ingredients and stir vigorously with wooden spoon until well combined.
3. Drop by tablespoonsful onto an ungreased nonstick cookie sheet.
4. Bake for 8 to 10 minutes, or until golden brown. Remove cookies from oven and cool on absorbent paper or wire rack.

................

Variations:

Easy Raisin-Walnut Cookies: *Prepare Basic Sugar Cookie dough and stir in 1 cup of raisins and $\frac{1}{2}$ cup chopped walnuts before baking.*

Easy Apricot-Pecan Cookies: *Prepare Basic Sugar Cookie dough and stir in 1 cup diced dried apricots and $\frac{1}{2}$ cup chopped pecans before baking.*

Easy Peanut Butter Cookies: *Prepare Basic Sugar Cookie dough, substituting $\frac{1}{2}$ cup creamy peanut butter for the margarine.*

................

# Low-Fat Chocolate Chewy Cookie Bars

2 cups reduced-fat biscuit mix
¼ cup powdered
      unsweetened cocoa
      (for baking)
¾ cup sugar
1 jar (8 ounces) pureed prunes
1 egg
½ cup nonfat milk
cooking oil spray

*Nothing beats chocolate when you have a sweet tooth, and these cookies will satisfy the cravings (with fewer calories and less fat).*

Estimated preparation time: 3 minutes
Estimated baking time: 20 minutes
Makes 1 dozen cookie bars

1. Preheat oven to 350 degrees.
2. Place biscuit mix, cocoa, and sugar into medium bowl and stir to combine. Add pureed prunes, egg, and milk, and stir vigorously with wooden spoon until mixture is creamed.
3. Lightly coat $9 \times 9$-inch nonstick baking dish with cooking oil spray, and spread batter in dish.
4. Bake for 20 minutes. Remove from oven, cool, and slice into bars.

# Easiest Boston Cream Pie

*This recipe was served to nearly twenty hungry musicians who insisted it could not be low fat—it is.*

Estimated preparation time: 10 minutes
Makes 8 servings

1. Slice pound cake horizontally into 3 layers. Place bottom layer on serving dish.
2. Gently beat pudding mix and milk in medium bowl until pudding begins to thicken.
3. Spoon half the pudding mixture over the bottom cake layer and top with second cake layer. Spoon remaining pudding mixture onto middle cake layer, and place final cake layer on top.
4. Place chocolate baking chips and water in 2-cup glass measuring cup. Microwave on high for 45 seconds. Whisk briskly with fork until smooth.
5. Pour melted chocolate over all three cake layers, allowing some of the chocolate to drizzle down the sides. Refrigerate until ready to serve.

1 purchased reduced-fat or nonfat pound cake
1 package (3.4 ounces) fat-free instant vanilla pudding mix
1 cup skim milk, chilled
½ cup reduced-fat semisweet chocolate baking chips
2 tablespoons water

Baking **167**

# Heavenly Chocolate Cherry Cake

1 ready-made angel food cake
    (10 to 12 inches)
1 cup nonfat whipped topping
1 package (8 ounces) nonfat
    cream cheese, softened
½ cup reduced-fat chocolate
    baking chips
2 tablespoons water
1 can (20 ounces) light cherry
    pie filling

*My oldest son chose the name for this recipe as he licked his dessert plate clean.*

Estimated preparation time: 15 minutes
Makes 12 servings

1. Cut cake into bite-sized pieces and place in large mixing bowl.
2. Place whipped topping and cream cheese in full-sized food processor and pulse until blended. Allow to sit while you prepare the chocolate.
3. Pour chocolate baking chips into 2-cup measuring cup, add water, and microwave on high for 45 seconds. Whisk melted chocolate with fork until smooth.
4. Immediately pour chocolate sauce over the cream cheese mixture in food processor and pulse until smooth and creamy.
5. Pour chocolate-cheese mixture over angel food cake pieces. Add cherry pie filling, and gently fold all ingredients together until well combined.
6. Spread mixture evenly in $9 \times 13$-inch baking dish. Refrigerate until ready to serve. Top with additional nonfat whipped topping, if desired.

# Sinfully Low-Fat Chocolate Cheesecake

*No one will believe that this rich, fudgy cheesecake has less than 5 grams of fat per slice—and if you don't tell them, they'll never know.*

Estimated preparation time: 8 minutes
Estimated refrigeration time: 1 hour
Makes 8 to 10 servings

1. Place cream cheese, sweetened condensed milk, and whipped topping in full-sized food processor. Pulse until smooth. Slowly add pudding mix, pulsing to blend.
2. Pour cream cheese mixture into pie shell. Refrigerate for at least 1 hour before serving. Top with dollop of additional nonfat whipped topping if desired.

1 package (8 ounces) nonfat cream cheese, softened
1 can (8 ounces) nonfat sweetened condensed milk
1 cup nonfat whipped topping, thawed
1 package (3.4 ounces) nonfat instant chocolate pudding mix
1 ready-made chocolate cookie pie shell

# Fast and Low-Fat Pumpkin Pie

1 package (3.4 ounces) nonfat instant vanilla pudding mix
1 cup nonfat whipped topping, thawed
½ cup skim milk
1 cup canned pumpkin
1½ teaspoons pumpkin pie spice
1 purchased reduced-fat graham cracker pie shell

*Replace your standard pumpkin pie recipe with this one, and you'll free up oven space for a larger turkey.*

Estimated preparation time: 5 minutes
Estimated refrigeration time: 1 hour
Makes 8 to 10 servings

1. Place pudding mix, whipped topping, milk, pumpkin, and pumpkin pie spice in medium bowl. Using an electric mixer, beat on low speed until smooth.
2. Pour pumpkin mixture into graham cracker pie shell and refrigerate for at least 1 hour before serving. Top with dollop of additional nonfat whipped topping, if desired.

# Easiest Apple "Crisp" Pie

*Everyone loves this super-simple pie—your family will, too.*

Estimated preparation time: 15 minutes
Estimated refrigeration time: 1 hour
Makes 8 generous servings

1. Place apple pie filling in medium glass bowl, gently stir in water, and microwave on high for 2 minutes. Stir. Microwave on high for an additional 1 to 2 minutes.
2. Sprinkle unflavored gelatin over hot apple mixture and stir until dissolved. Allow to cool slightly, then pour warm apple mixture into pie shell, spreading evenly. Sprinkle granola on top. Refrigerate for 1 to 2 hours before serving.

1 can (20 ounces) light apple pie filling
½ cup water
1 envelope (2 ounces) un-flavored gelatin
1 purchased reduced-fat graham cracker pie shell
¾ cup low-fat granola cereal

# Fruit and Easy Mousse

1 package (8 ounces) nonfat
    cream cheese, softened
1 container (8 ounces) nonfat
    whipped topping,
    thawed
1 cup nonfat lemon flavored
    yogurt
1 package (3.4 ounces) nonfat
    instant lemon pudding
    mix
2 cups fresh berries (such as
    blueberries,
    raspberries,
    strawberries)

*It tastes sweet and decadent, but this no-bake dessert is packed with nutrition.*

Estimated preparation time: 10 minutes
Estimated refrigeration time: 1 hour
Makes 6 to 8 servings.

1. Place cream cheese, whipped topping, and yogurt into full-sized food processor and pulse until smooth. Slowly add pudding mix, pulsing until well blended.
2. Remove blade from food processor and gently fold in fresh berries with spatula.
3. Spoon mousse mixture into small dessert bowls. Refrigerate for at least 1 hour before serving.

# 9
# SNACKS

Fat-Free White Bean Dip
Tomato Cheese Dip
Carefree Cheese and
  "Crab" Dip
Deviled Ham and Cheese
  Dip
Dump-Style Homemade
  Salsa
Quick, Fresh Snack Bowl
Crunchy Cracker-
  Sandwich Bites

Peanut Butter Pinwheel
  Treats
Savory Party Mix
Power-Snack Popcorn
Cheesy Circle Snack Mix
Colorful Corn Tortilla
  Bowl
Barbecue Meatballs and
  Mini-Rolls
Streamlined Fruit-and-
  Veggie Tray

I admit . . . we don't stock a lot of potato chips, packaged snacks, or other munchies in our pantry. It wasn't always that way, but several years ago—at over 200 pounds—I realized that those tasty treats weren't doing me or my family any good. In my own efforts to lose weight and get back in shape, I didn't want my husband or children to feel deprived. So I began making healthier munchies we could all enjoy freely.

Nothing beats chips, veggies, and dips when last-minute company pops in, so you'll find recipes for delicious entertaining in this chapter. You'll also find recipes for tempting appetizers that double as healthy after-school snacks. When you want to munch on the run, you'll find ideas for quick and easy nibbles you throw together using basic pantry items, and there are even recipes for large gatherings or parties.

# Fat-Free White Bean Dip

*My guys love this creamy, lowfat dip, and you can use it in place of refried beans for many recipes.*

Estimated preparation time: 5 minutes
Makes about 2¼ cups

1. Puree beans in food processor.
2. Add onion, garlic, cumin, and lemon juice. Pulse to combine. Season with salt and pepper.
3. Serve hot or cold. Refrigerate for up to 5 days.

1 can (19 ounces) white beans, rinsed and drained
1 medium white onion, finely chopped
1 clove garlic, minced
¼ teaspoon cumin
1 tablespoon lemon juice
salt and pepper

Snacks

**175**

# Tomato Cheese Dip

1 pound reduced-fat processed
cheese spread, cubed
1 can (10 ounces) diced
tomatoes and chilies

*This is not quite as spicy, salty, or "fatty" as standard nacho dips, but it tastes great!*

Estimated preparation time: 5 minutes
Makes about 2½ cups

1. Place ingredients in microwavable covered dish. Microwave on high, stirring once, until cheese melts, about 2 minutes.
2. Serve immediately. Refrigerate remainder for up to 3 days, and reheat to serve.

# Carefree Cheese and "Crab" Dip

*Planning a dinner party? Be sure to include this winning recipe!*

Estimated preparation time: 5 minutes
Makes about 2 cups dip

1. Place all ingredients in food processor and pulse until creamy.
2. Transfer to small serving bowl, cover, and refrigerate until ready to serve. Consume within 3 days.

. . . . . . . . . . . . . . . .

Note: You can also serve this dip in the center of a platter with baked whole wheat crackers and fresh vegetables for a cool, light summer dinner.

. . . . . . . . . . . . . . . .

1 package (8 ounces) imitation crab meat
1 cup nonfat creamed cottage cheese
2 tablespoons nonfat plain yogurt or sour cream
1 tablespoon lemon juice
½ teaspoon garlic powder
2 sprigs fresh dill

# Deviled Ham and Cheese Dip

1 can (4.5 ounces) deviled ham
1 container (4 ounces) nonfat cream cheese spread
½ cup nonfat plain yogurt
6 to 8 pimiento-stuffed olives

*Holidays are a wonderful time to wow your family and friends with this simple dip.*

Estimated preparation time: 5 minutes
Makes about 1½ cups

1. Place all ingredients in food processor and pulse until smooth.
2. Transfer to small serving bowl, cover, and refrigerate until ready to use. Consume within 3 days.

. . . . . . . . . . . . . . . . .

Note: Serve it with fresh vegetables and bread sticks for a quick, springtime snack.

. . . . . . . . . . . . . . . . .

# Dump-Style Homemade Salsa

*Not all bottled salsas meet everyone's tastes. With this less expensive, "homemade" version, you can use more or less chili powder to control heat—remember, the spice intensifies after a day or two.*

1 can (15 ounces) diced
  tomatoes, drained
1 can (6 ounces) diced green
  chilies, drained
½ cup diced onion (fresh or
  frozen)
½ teaspoon minced garlic
½ to 1 teaspoon chili powder

Estimated preparation time: 5 minutes
Makes about 2⅔ cups

1. Place all ingredients into small bowl and toss well to combine.
2. Cover and refrigerate for up to 1 week.

# Quick, Fresh Snack Bowl

1 small bunch seedless white
    or green grapes
1 small bunch seedless red
    grapes
2 medium apples, cored and
    sliced into wedges
2 oranges, seeded, peeled, and
    separated into wedges
4 ounces reduced-fat cheddar
    cheese, cut into small
    cubes
4 ounces reduced-fat
    Monterey Jack cheese,
    cut into small cubes

*Assemble this nutritious mix and refrigerate for after-school snacking, or bring a double batch to your child's classroom party.*

Estimated preparation time: 10 minutes
Makes 4 servings

1. Place all ingredients in medium bowl—toss together, or arrange by type—and serve.

# Crunchy Cracker-Sandwich Bites

*Your children can make their own cracker sandwiches using two crackers, a piece of cheese, and a vegetable round for each—try them in lunches, too.*

16 whole wheat crackers
16 saltine crackers
4 slices 2%-fat American cheese, each cut into four equal pieces
1 medium zucchini or cucumber, sliced into thin rounds

Estimated preparation time: 7 minutes
Makes 4 servings

1. Arrange crackers, cheese, and zucchini or cucumber on serving platter.
2. Serve immediately, allowing people to put together their own sandwiches. If not serving immediately, cover and refrigerate until ready.

# Peanut Butter Pinwheel Treats

4 flour tortillas (8 inch)
4 tablespoons chunky peanut
    butter
2 tablespoons unsweetened
    applesauce

*Preschoolers love this easy snack.*

Estimated preparation time: 10 minutes
Makes 3 to 4 servings

1. Put tortillas between damp paper towels and micro-wave on high for 20 seconds to warm.
2. Blend peanut butter and applesauce in small bowl until smooth, and spread evenly on each tortilla.
3. Layer two tortillas by placing one on top of another, peanut butter side up. Roll and refrigerate for at least 10 minutes. Slice into 1-inch segments and serve.

. . . . . . . . . . . . . . . .

Note: you can store Peanut Butter Pinwheel Treats in sandwich bags in the refrigerator for a quick lunch-box surprise.

. . . . . . . . . . . . . . . .

# Savory Party Mix

*Almost everyone loves Chex brand party mix, and this lower fat alternative is just as delicious.*

Estimated preparation time: 3 minutes
Estimated cooking time: 5 to 6 minutes
Makes about 12 servings

4 cups shredded wheat cereal nuggets
1 cup small unsalted pretzels
1 cup popped popcorn
3 tablespoons margarine, melted
1 tablespoon Worcestershire sauce
1 teaspoon seasoned salt

1. Mix cereal, pretzels, and popcorn in large microwavable bowl.
2. Whisk together margarine, Worcestershire sauce, and seasoned salt in small bowl. Drizzle evenly over dry mixture, tossing to coat evenly.
3. Microwave on high for 3 minutes, and stir. Microwave for 2 to 3 minutes, or until crisp.
4. Remove from microwave and allow to cool. Store in tightly sealed container.

# Power-Snack Popcorn

1 bag (3.5 ounces) regular
    microwavable popcorn
$\frac{1}{4}$ teaspoon cayenne pepper
$\frac{3}{4}$ teaspoon ground cumin
$\frac{3}{4}$ teaspoon salt
$\frac{1}{2}$ teaspoon garlic powder
$1\frac{1}{2}$ cups peanuts, preferably
    honey-roasted
$1\frac{1}{2}$ cups raisins

*We eat lots of popcorn in our home, but the boys get tired of the same old snack. The seasonings, peanuts, and raisins make this a favorite play-date treat.*

Estimated preparation time: 15 minutes
Makes about 16 cups

1. Pop popcorn according to package directions and place in large bowl.
2. Sprinkle with cayenne, cumin, salt, and garlic powder, and toss to coat evenly. Stir in peanuts and raisins.

# Cheesy Circle Snack Mix

*This unusual mix was another winning "accident" on a rushed afternoon—you can substitute other unsweetened cereals with similar results.*

2 cups toasted oats cereal
2 cups corn puff cereal
2 tablespoons reduced-fat
    Caesar dressing

Estimated preparation time: 3 minutes
Estimated cooking time: 2 minutes
Makes 4 cups

1. Place cereal in 1-gallon plastic storage bag. Drizzle dressing over cereal, seal, and shake vigorously.
2. Microwave sealed bag on high for 2 minutes.
3. Remove bag from oven, shake bag again, and pour seasoned mix into serving bowl.

# Colorful Corn Tortilla Bowl

2 bags (12 ounces each) white
    corn tortilla chips
2 bags (12 ounces each) blue
    corn tortilla chips
Fat-Free White Bean Dip
    (recipe, page 175)
Dump-Style Homemade Salsa
    (recipe, page 179)

*This is an ideal treat for informal parties, and can also act as lunch during the weekend—be sure to have plenty on hand for the big game.*

Estimated preparation time: 10 minutes
Makes 12 servings

1. Combine chips in large bowl.
2. Prepare the two dips and serve.

Snacks

# Barbecue Meatballs and Mini-Rolls

*This "snack" is more like a meal, and when your crew is hungry, they'll love it.*

Estimated preparation time: 5 minutes
Estimated cooking time: 10 minutes
Makes 12 rolls

1 package (16 ounces) frozen cooked meatballs
1 cup bottled barbecue sauce (any variety)
12 French-style rolls, cut in half lengthwise

1. Place meatballs and sauce in medium nonstick pot. Cook over medium-low heat for 10 minutes, stirring occasionally.
2. Transfer to platter or serving bowl. Serve with rolls to make quick meatball sandwiches.

. . . . . . . . . . . . . . . .

Note: If you don't have French rolls on hand, use prepared biscuits to make up to 20 mini-sandwiches.

. . . . . . . . . . . . . . . .

# Streamlined Fruit-and-Veggie Tray

1 pint fresh strawberries or
   raspberries
¾ pound seedless white or
   green grapes
1 pint cherry tomatoes
1 pint fresh broccoli florets
1 bag (16 ounces) baby carrots
1 cup nonfat ranch dressing

*Fruit and vegetable trays are undoubtedly healthy, but cutting and dicing are a lot of work—let the grocer do your work for you, and relax.*

Estimated preparation time: 5 minutes
Makes 12 servings

1. Arrange fruit and vegetables on serving platter.
2. Pour dressing into small bowl and place in center of the platter. Serve.

# 10
# GUEST-PLEASING
# GOURMET

Terrific and Easy Trifle
Two-Grocery-Bag Party
Freezer Section Party Fare
Easy Freezer Dessert
Christmas in a Hurry
Black Forest Chocolate
    Cheesecake
Amazing Easter Dinner
Amazing Blackberry Pyra-
    mid Cake
Easy New Year's Brunch
Quick and Kosher Holiday
    Dinner

Last-Minute Sweet and
    Sour Shrimp
Last-Minute Creamy
    "Crab" Roll-ups
Last-Minute Beefy Barbe-
    cue Wraps
Last-Minute Hawaiian
    Pizza
Last-Minute Baked Maca-
    roni and Cheese
Speedy Southwestern
    Dinner
Almost-Catered Chicken
    Dinner

I've been cooking for more than twenty years, so family and friends have come to expect "better than basics" food when I entertain (and I entertain as often as possible). I'm a very busy working mom. I don't always have time to prepare complicated dishes—and thanks to new supermarket items, I don't have to. Neither do you! "Gourmet" no longer has to mean you spent hours in the kitchen; it means you made something special out of basic fare.

This chapter will show you how to impress your guests with simple party recipes. You'll also find recipes for fast, full-course holiday meals. When friends pop in unexpectedly, you'll be ready to roll with last-minute magic tricks—and for large, planned celebrations you'll find entire menus for not-quite-catered success.

# Terrific and Easy Trifle

*Trifles are not only easy to prepare, they look fabulous—this one is sure to be a favorite with your guests.*

Estimated preparation time: 7 minutes
Makes 16 to 18 servings

1. Slightly crush the cookies by removing inner bag from box, shaking vigorously, and applying gentle pressure. Place half of the crushed cookies in the bottom of a clear, large serving bowl.
2. Spoon pudding onto cookies, and add another layer of cookies on the pudding. Top with pie filling.
3. Cover and refrigerate until ready to serve.

1 package (16 ounces) vanilla wafers
1 quart prepared chocolate pudding (from grocery deli)
1 can (16 ounces) light cherry pie filling

# Two-Grocery-Bag Party

cooking oil spray
8 russet potatoes, halved
    lengthwise
6 lamb rib chops
6 pork sausage links
6 marinated boneless, skinless
    chicken breasts
1 bunch fresh rosemary,
    leaves stripped from
    stems
4 to 6 portobello mushrooms,
    halved
2 packages (16 ounces each)
    salad greens
salad dressing

*An entire party in two grocery bags? Absolutely! You can feed up to eighteen guests with this menu: Serve meats, potatoes, mushrooms, and salad with fresh fruit, fresh bread from the grocery bakery, and beverages of your choice. For dessert, serve Terrific and Easy Trifle, page 191.*

Estimated preparation time: 15 minutes
Estimated cooking time: 24 minutes
Makes 16 to 18 servings

1. Preheat broiler. Lightly coat broiling pan and nonstick cookie sheet with cooking oil spray.
2. Place potatoes cut side up in microwave oven and microwave on high for 10 minutes. Allow to sit in microwave.
3. Arrange chops, sausages, and chicken breasts on broiler pan. Sprinkle chops with fresh rosemary leaves.
4. Arrange partially cooked potatoes cut-side down on cookie sheet. Arrange mushrooms on cookie sheet and broiler pan (so that all items can fit on 2 pans in 1 small oven).
5. Place cookie sheet on bottom rack in oven. Place broiler pan on middle rack of oven. Close oven door and broil for 7 minutes; slide middle rack out enough

to turn the meats, slide back into place, and broil for an additional 5 minutes.

6. Turn oven off, remove broiler pan and cookie sheet, and arrange meats, potatoes, and mushrooms on two large platters.

7. Place salad greens in a large serving bowl and drizzle with your favorite dressing.

# Freezer Section Party Fare

*Sandwiches:*

2 packages (9 ounces each) frozen stuffed Philly steak and cheese sandwiches (such as Lean Pockets brand)

2 packages (9 ounces each) frozen stuffed ham and cheese sandwiches (such as Lean Pockets brand)

2 packages (9 ounces each) frozen stuffed turkey and ham with cheddar sandwiches (such as Lean Pockets brand)

⅓ cup nonfat Italian dressing

*Potatoes:*

2 packages (16 ounces each) frozen O'Brian-style diced potatoes (with onions and peppers)

⅔ cup reduced-fat mayonnaise

¼ cup prepared mustard

*Grab all of the ingredients at the supermarket, and your party will be ready any time. Serve with tossed, green salad and Easy Freezer Dessert, which follows this recipe.*

Estimated preparation time: 10 minutes
Estimated cooking time: 22 minutes
Makes 12 servings

1. Preheat oven to 425 degrees.
2. Remove frozen sandwiches from wrappers and arrange on 2 nonstick cookie sheets. Brush with Italian dressing and place on center rack of hot oven. Reduce heat to 350 degrees and bake for 12 minutes. Remove from oven and allow to cool slightly.
3. Fork-puncture frozen bags of potatoes, place one at a time in microwave oven, and microwave on high for 6 minutes each.
4. Remove potatoes from bags and place in large serving bowl. Add mayonnaise and mustard and toss well.

Note: You can cut your cooking time in half by starting the potato salad while the sandwiches are baking.

# Easy Freezer Dessert

*This is one of the easiest desserts you'll ever make. Serve the berries that top this waffle whole, or puree them for a quick sauce.*

12 frozen reduced-fat waffles
½ gallon vanilla frozen yogurt
1 package (12 ounces) frozen
berries, thawed

Estimated preparation time: 10 minutes
Estimated cooking time: 5 to 8 minutes
Makes 12 servings

1. Lightly toast waffles (or warm in 350-degree oven for 5 minutes).
2. Top each waffle with a scoop of frozen yogurt and 1 tablespoon thawed berries; serve immediately.

# Christmas in a Hurry

*Turkey:*

1 whole smoked turkey (12 to 14 pounds)

*Sweet Potatoes:*

cooking oil spray
2 cans (16 ounces each) sweet potatoes, drained
2 jars (8 ounces each) pureed apricots
¼ cup brown sugar, loosely packed

*Creamed Spinach:*

1 package (16 ounces) frozen chopped spinach, thawed
1 can (10.75 ounces) reduced-fat condensed cream of mushroom soup
1 cup crushed cornflakes

*Stuffing:*

2 packages (10 ounces each) complete stovetop stuffing mix
1 cup raisins

*Make the most of this meal by asking your children to assist you in the preparation. Serve this Christmas dinner with tossed salad, fresh rolls, and Black Forest Chocolate Cheesecake (page 197).*

Estimated preparation time: 30 minutes
Estimated baking time: 1 hour
Makes 12 servings

1. Preheat oven to 350 degrees.
2. Prepare the turkey: Place smoked whole turkey in large roasting pan, cover with foil, and bake at 350 degrees for 1 hour, or until thoroughly heated.
3. Prepare the sweet potatoes: Lightly coat casserole dish with cooking oil spray. Add canned sweet potatoes and apricot puree. Sprinkle brown sugar on top. Cover, add to preheated oven, and cook for 20 to 25 minutes.
4. Prepare the spinach: Lightly coat microwavable casserole dish with cooking oil spray. Add thawed spinach and condensed soup, and stir. Cover and microwave on high for 12 minutes. Stir. Sprinkle with crushed cornflakes and microwave uncovered on high for an additional 3 to 4 minutes, or until sauce begins to bubble. Remove from microwave, cover, and let sit.
5. Prepare the stuffing: Prepare mix according to package directions. Stir in raisins before serving.

# Black Forest Chocolate Cheesecake

*This festive recipe bakes longer than many recipes in this cookbook, but it's definitely worth it. For a larger crowd, bake two at the same time.*

Estimated preparation time: 15 minutes
Estimated baking time: 45 minutes
Estimated refrigeration time: 1 hour
Makes 8 medium or 10 small servings

2 packages (8 ounces each) cream cheese, softened
1 can (14 ounces) chocolate sweetened condensed milk (not evaporated milk)
3 eggs
1 prepared chocolate cookie pie crust
1 can (21 ounces) cherry pie filling, chilled

1. Preheat oven to 350 degrees.
2. Beat the cream cheese in large bowl until fluffy. Gradually beat in sweetened condensed milk until mixture is smooth. Add eggs and mix well.
3. Pour mixture into pie crust and bake for 45 minutes, or until center is set. Allow to cool, then refrigerate at least 1 hour. Top with cherry pie filling before serving.

# Amazing Easter Dinner

*Ham:*

1 fully cooked whole ham,
  bone in (8 to 10
  pounds)
1 can (13.25 ounces)
  pineapple chunks,
  drained
1 can (16 ounces) apricot
  halves, drained
1 cup bottled sweet and sour
  sauce

*Sweet Potatoes:*

2 cans (16 ounces each) sweet
  potatoes, drained
1 teaspoon cinnamon
$\frac{2}{3}$ cup nonfat milk
2 tablespoons margarine

*Vegetables:*

1 package (16 ounces) frozen
  specialty peas and baby
  carrots, thawed

*Simplicity assures holiday success, and this Easter dinner couldn't be simpler. Serve with tossed salad, fresh bread, and Amazing Blackberry Pyramid Cake (opposite).*

Estimated preparation time: 25 minutes
Estimated baking time: 1 hour
Makes 12 servings

1. Preheat oven to 350 degrees.
2. Prepare the ham: Place ham in large roasting pan, add pineapple and apricots, and pour sweet and sour sauce over all. Bake for 1 hour, or until heated thoroughly.
3. Prepare the sweet potatoes: Place sweet potatoes, cinnamon, and milk in food processor and pulse until smooth. Transfer to microwavable casserole dish, drop margarine in center, cover, and microwave on high for 10 to 12 minutes.
4. Prepare the vegetables: Place thawed peas and baby carrots in medium nonstick pot. Add $\frac{1}{3}$ cup water, cover, and simmer over medium low heat for 15 minutes, stirring occasionally.

# Amazing Blackberry Pyramid Cake

*Your guests will think you baked for hours to make this special cake, and it tastes as great as it looks!*

Estimated preparation time: 20 minutes
Makes 12 servings

1. Trim the top, bottom, and sides off the pound cake to make sharp edges. (Take your time: If the cake isn't trimmed neatly, the result will be a lumpy—rather than stunning—dessert.)
2. Slice cake horizontally into quarters.
3. Spread 3 tablespoons preserves on three of the four cake layers.
4. Align the long edge of the bottom layer at the edge of a countertop. Stack layers to form a layered cake.
5. Using a long, serrated knife held at a 45-degree angle to the countertop, slice the layered cake in half (the end of the knife should extend through the cake out past the edge of the countertop—use the countertop edge as a cutting guide)—you'll have two long, triangular pieces. Place the triangular pieces "back to back" to form a long pyramid, so that the filling of the layers shows vertical.
6. Spread the remaining preserves between the two halves to form the final layer. Frost with whipped topping and refrigerate until ready to serve.

1 package (16 ounces) frozen pound cake, thawed
1 cup plus 2 tablespoons blackberry preserves
1 cup frozen nonfat whipped topping, thawed

# Easy New Year's Brunch

*Pancake Rolls:*

16 frozen buttermilk pancakes
16 precooked pork sausage
    links (or kielbasa links)
2 cups reduced-fat cottage
    cheese
½ cup light maple syrup

*Potatoes:*

cooking oile spray
1 package (16 ounces) fresh
    shredded potatoes (or
    frozen, thawed)
½ cup chopped onion (fresh
    or frozen)
½ cup chopped green pepper
    (fresh or frozen)
¼ cup chopped, fresh parsley,
    or 2 tablespoons dried
    parsley flakes
3 containers (4 ounces each)
    egg substitute, thawed
⅔ cup nonfat milk

*Fruit Dessert:*

1 can (16 ounces) light apple
    pie filling
1 can (16 ounces) light cherry
    pie filling
1½ cups dried apricots
½ cup currants
whipped cream (optional)

*I often prefer a casual brunch to a fancy dinner party, and New Year's Day is the perfect time to host one. The following menu will start your year successfully.*

Estimated preparation time: 20 minutes
Estimated baking time: 20 minutes
Makes 12 servings

1. Preheat oven to 350 degrees.
2. Prepare the pancakes: Place frozen pancakes between slightly damp paper towels and microwave on high for 30 seconds. Rearrange order of pancakes, return to microwave, and heat on high for an additional 30 seconds. Continue until all pancakes are warm and pliable (about 2 minutes).
3. Roll sausages in pancakes and arrange (seam-side down) in $9 \times 13$-inch foil baking pans. Cover with foil and set aside on counter.
4. Place cottage cheese and maple syrup in small bowl, stir to combine, cover, and refrigerate. Spoon 1 tablespoon sweetened cottage cheese onto center of each pancake roll before serving.
5. Prepare the potatoes: Lightly coat another $9 \times 13$-inch baking pan with cooking oil spray. Spread shredded potatoes evenly on the bottom of pan. Sprinkle onion,

green pepper, and parsley over potatoes. Place egg substitute and milk in medium bowl and whisk together. Pour over potatoes.

6. Place all three baking pans in preheated oven and bake for 20 minutes. Remove from oven, cool slightly, and slice into 12 equal portions.

7. Prepare the fruit dessert: Pour pie fillings in medium nonstick pot. Stir in dried fruits and cook over low heat for 10 to 12 minutes, stirring occasionally. When mixture begins to bubble, cover and remove from heat. Serve with whipped cream if desired.

# Quick and Kosher Holiday Dinner

*Beef:*

1 whole beef tenderloin (5 to 6 pounds)
2 tablespoons extra virgin olive oil
1 small bunch fresh rosemary
1 small bunch fresh thyme

*Rice:*

1 cup white rice
1 cup wild rice
½ cup dried cranberries
½ cup chopped pecans
2 cans (10.75 ounces each) chicken broth
½ cup orange juice
2 tablespoons honey

*Salad:*

2 packages (16 ounces each) salad greens
salad dressing

*This is a fast, easy, and delicious meal for any number of holidays.*

Estimated preparation time: 20 minutes
Estimated baking time: 1 hour
Makes 12 servings

1. Preheat oven to 375 degrees.
2. Prepare the beef: With very clean hands, place beef tenderloin on large sheet of heavy duty aluminum foil (shiny side up) and brush with oil. Arrange fresh herbs on top of meat. Wrap tightly in foil, place in medium roasting pan, and cover. Turn heat down to 350 degrees and bake for 1 hour. Remove from oven and allow to sit for 15 minutes before unwrapping and carving. Meat will be rare.
3. Prepare the rice: Combine rice, cranberries, pecans, broth, orange juice, and honey in a microwavable 2-quart casserole dish. Cover and microwave on high for 20 minutes, stirring and turning once during cooking.
4. Prepare the salad: Place salad greens in large bowl and drizzle with dressing of your choice.

Note: Beef tenderloin tastes best when cooked rare; exercise caution when handling raw meat.

Guest-Pleasing Gourmet

# Last-Minute Sweet and Sour Shrimp

*With a dash to the grocery store for items you might not have on hand, and three minutes preparation time, it's easy to entertain improvisationally. Serve this to your last-minute guests with a fresh salad.*

Estimated preparation. time: 3 minutes
Estimated cooking time: 15 minutes
Makes 8 servings

1. Place all ingredients in a large, nonstick pot.
2. Cook over medium-high heat, stirring occasionally, until liquid begins to bubble.
3. Reduce heat to lowest setting, cover, and cook for an additional 10 minutes. Serve.

2 cups uncooked instant rice
1½ cups water
2 tablespoons lemon juice
1 tablespoon reduced-sodium soy sauce
2 tablespoons apricot preserves or seedless raspberry preserves
1 package (6 ounces) frozen cooked shrimp
1 package (16 ounces) frozen broccoli stir-fry vegetable mix (broccoli, carrots, onions, red peppers, celery, water chestnuts, mushrooms)

# Last-Minute Creamy "Crab" Roll-ups

1 package (6 ounces) imitation crab meat, diced
1 package (8 ounces) reduced-fat cream cheese, cubed
2 scallions, finely diced
1 medium tomato, finely diced
8 flour tortillas (8 inch)
cooking oil spray
nonfat sour cream (optional)

*When company drops by unexpectedly, make this fast, simple meal. Serve with canned or fresh fruit.*

Estimated preparation time: 8 minutes
Estimated baking time: 12 minutes
Makes 8 servings

1. Preheat oven to 375 degrees.
2. Arrange imitation crab meat, cream cheese cubes, and vegetables evenly on each flour tortilla. Carefully roll the tortillas enchilada-style.
3. Lightly coat $9 \times 13$-inch baking dish with cooking oil spray. Arrange roll-ups in dish.
4. Bake for 12 minutes, or until tortillas are just beginning to turn golden brown. Top with nonfat sour cream, if desired.

# Last-Minute Beefy Barbecue Wraps

*This is a wonderful "company" meal when served with coleslaw and Spanish rice from your grocery deli.*

2 cups chopped cooked beef
    (leftovers work well)
8 flour tortillas (8 inch)
½ cup barbecue sauce
½ cup diced green peppers
    (fresh or frozen)
1 cup reduced-fat shredded
    cheddar cheese
cooking oil spray

Estimated preparation time: 10 minutes
Estimated baking time: 10 to 12 minutes
Makes 8 servings

1. Preheat oven to 350 degrees.
2. Arrange beef in center of each tortilla. Spoon 1 tablespoon barbecue sauce over meat, then sprinkle with green peppers and cheese.
3. Lightly coat $9 \times 13$-inch baking pan with cooking oil spray. Roll tortillas enchilada-style and place seam-side down in baking dish.
4. Bake for 10 to 12 minutes, or until cheese melts.

# Last-Minute Hawaiian Pizza

2 prepared pizza shells
    (12 inch)
2 medium tomatoes, sliced
    very thin
2 pounds cooked ham, cut
    into thin strips or deli
    sliced
2 small onions, sliced very
    thin
2 cans (6 ounces each) pine-
    apple chunks, drained
3 cups reduced-fat shredded
    mozzarella cheese

*If your friends and family have hearty appetites, consider making a second pizza by spreading canned chili on a pizza shell and sprinkling with cheddar cheese—the flavors work well together.*

Estimated preparation time: 10 minutes
Estimated baking time: 12 minutes
Makes 6 servings

1. Preheat oven to 400 degrees.
2. Place pizza shells on cookie sheet or pizza pan. Arrange tomato slices on pizza shells, then lay strips of ham over tomato slices. Top with onion slices, pineapple chunks, and shredded cheese.
3. Bake for 12 minutes, or until cheese bubbles.

# Last-Minute Baked Macaroni and Cheese

*This is the perfect "grab it on your way home" meal for a crowd. Serve with a simple tossed salad and fresh bread.*

1 package (4 to 5 pounds) frozen macaroni and cheese (party size)
1 cup plain dry bread crumbs
½ cup grated Romano cheese
¼ cup chopped fresh parsley

Estimated preparation time: 3 minutes
Estimated baking time: varies according to brand
Makes 12 generous servings

1. Bake macaroni and cheese according to package directions.
2. Combine remaining ingredients in a small bowl.
3. When the macaroni and cheese is ready, sprinkle bread crumb mixture over it and bake for another 5 minutes, or until bread crumbs turn golden brown.

# Speedy Southwestern Dinner

1 package (12 ounces) frozen cooked beef for fajitas
1 package (12 ounces) frozen cooked chicken breast for fajitas
1 green pepper, sliced into thin strips
1 red pepper, sliced into thin strips
1 medium onion, sliced into thin strips and halved
½ pint cherry tomatoes, halved
1½ pounds prepared Spanish rice (from grocery deli)
2 cans (15 ounces each) seasoned pinto beans, drained
8 flour tortillas (8 inch)

*This easy-to-assemble menu goes from grocery bag to dinner table in twenty-seven minutes.*

Estimated preparation time: 15 minutes
Estimated cooking time: 12 minutes
Makes 8 servings.

1. Preheat oven to 375 degrees.
2. Place frozen meat, sliced peppers, and onion on a nonstick cookie sheet. Slide cookie sheet onto center rack of oven and heat for 10 minutes. Add cherry tomatoes and heat for 2 minutes longer.
3. Place rice in medium-sized microwavable bowl. Cover, and microwave on high about 3 minutes to reheat.
4. Place beans in medium microwavable bowl. Microwave on high about 4 minutes or until thoroughly heated.
5. Microwave tortillas on high about 1 minute to warm. Assemble fajitas. Serve with hot rice and beans.

• • • • • • • • • • • • • • • •

Note: If your children won't eat bell pepper strips, experiment with other vegetables, such as thinly sliced zucchini and carrots.

• • • • • • • • • • • • • • • •

# Almost-Catered Chicken Dinner

*When you don't have time to cook, but don't have the budget to hire a caterer, this menu solves all of your problems.*

Estimated preparation time: 15 minutes
Estimated baking time: 20 to 25 minutes
Makes 8 to 10 servings

1. Prepare the chicken: Place chickens side by side in large roasting pan. Cover, place in cold oven, and set temperature for 375 degrees. Heat thoroughly, about 20 to 25 minutes.
2. Remove baked potatoes from their packaging, and microwave according to package directions. Transfer to cookie sheet. Drop 1 tablespoon cold soup onto each potato, place in oven with chicken, and heat until soup has melted, about __ minutes.
3. Prepare the coleslaw: Put coleslaw vegetables, raisins, and dressing in medium bowl. Toss until well combined. Sprinkle with sunflower seeds and refrigerate.
4. Heat the rolls, and serve with honey butter.

*Chicken:*

2 deli rotisserie chickens (3 to 4 pounds each)

*Potatoes:*

4 packages (10 ounces each) frozen baked potatoes (such as Twice Baked brand by Ore Ida)
1 can (10.75 ounces) reduced-fat condensed golden mushroom soup

*Coleslaw:*

1 package (16 ounces) broccoli coleslaw
1 cup raisins or currants
1 cup bottled coleslaw dressing
2 tablespoons roasted sunflower seeds

*Rolls:*

1 dozen fresh bakery rolls
1 tub (4 ounces) honey butter

# Additional Ideas for Fast Dinners

..................

Fabulous French Fare: *Impress your guests with heated and jazzed-up quiche from your grocery deli. Top a traditional spinach quiche with a large dollop of nonfat sour cream and a small sprig of fresh herbs.*

Nearly Take-Out Chinese: *Use frozen chicken nuggets or popcorn shrimp, bottled sweet and sour sauce, canned pineapple, and fresh or frozen vegetables over prepared instant rice. Purchase fortune cookies in the specialty section of your grocery store.*

Improvised Italian Dinner: *Look in the freezer section for stuffed manicotti, raviolis, lasagna roll-ups, and garlic bread. Add a jar of spaghetti sauce and a simple tossed salad.*

"Fast Food" Chicken Sandwiches and Fries: *Heat precooked, breaded chicken patties (or breast slices) and frozen, microwavable fries; with burger buns, lettuce, tomato, and condiments you can duplicate restaurant chain varieties.*

Savory Subs: *For no-cook success, purchase unusual loaves of bakery breads (for example, sun-dried tomato). Instead of the standard lettuce, tomato, and American cheese, try spinach leaves, fresh herbs, golden tomatoes, and crumbled feta over deli roast beef.*

..................

210                    Guest-Pleasing Gourmet

# 11
# CULINARY
# KIDS

Cheesy Fruit Parfaits
Easy Cheesy Waffle Sandwiches
Toasted Banana-Nut Pancakes
Quick Crunchy Porridge
Turkey Club Buns
Bologna Wrap Sandwiches
Golden Tuna Bagels
Brawny Beef Sub
Fruit and Tuna Salad Boats
Stuffed-Crust Pita Pizzas

Hot Diggity Dog Pie
Ravioli Casserole
Earthquake Taco Salad
Bread Bowl Chicken Taco Salad
Frozen Yogurt Pops
Chewy Oatmeal Bars
Rainbow Melon Wedges
Red, White, and Blue Graham Towers
Pecan Cookies

Kids in the kitchen are doing more than distracting you or making a mess—they're learning about basic chemistry, physics, and nutrition. When your children are involved in the preparation of a meal, they're also developing lifelong skills. The same four year old who dumped three times the necessary amount of salad dressing into the bowl might grow up to be the next Wolfgang Puck. More important, children who have the opportunity to cook by your side (or on their own) gain a sense of pride and significance.

This chapter contains kid-friendly recipes for quick and easy breakfasts, short-order lunches, simple and tasty dinners, and fabulously fast desserts. Each recipe is designed with the elementary school–aged child in mind, and you can assist younger children who wish to join in the fun.

# Cheesy Fruit Parfaits

*These creamy, nutritious parfaits are fun and easy to assemble.*

2 cups low-fat cottage cheese
1 can (16 ounces) light
    blueberry pie filling
1 cup low-fat granola without
    raisins

Estimated preparation time: 5 minutes
Makes 4 servings

1. Have your child spoon ½ cup cottage cheese into each of four small bowls.
2. Help your child divide the berry pie filling evenly between each of the bowls with a small slotted spoon.
3. Sprinkle ¼ cup granola on top of each parfait and serve.

Note: Consider using shatterproof serving bowls when preparing this with a small child.

# Easy Cheesy Waffle Sandwiches

8 frozen waffles, thawed, or
toasted and cooled
1 container (8 ounces)
reduced-fat whipped
cream cheese
4 tablespoons low-sugar fruit
spread

*Talk about an out-the-door breakfast! This recipe is ideal for days when your gang is in a rush.*

Estimated preparation time: 5 to 7 minutes
Makes 4 servings

1. Have your child spread 4 waffles with whipped cream cheese, and each of 4 waffles with 1 tablespoon fruit spread.
2. Assemble sandwiches, cut in half, and serve.

# Toasted Banana-Nut Pancakes

*These pancakes aren't cooked on a hot griddle, so even preschoolers can whip them up quickly and easily.*

4 frozen pancakes, toasted
2 bananas, sliced
½ cup chopped walnuts
4 teaspoons powdered sugar

Estimated preparation time: 5 to 7 minutes
Makes 4 servings

1. Have your child arrange banana slices on each pancake.
2. Sprinkle with nuts and sugar and serve.

# Quick Crunchy Porridge

4 cups low-fat granola
1 cup nonfat vanilla yogurt
$\frac{2}{3}$ cup nonfat milk

*This hearty breakfast cereal is warm and comforting on a chilly morning.*

Estimated preparation time: 3 minutes
Estimated cooking time: 3 minutes
Makes 4 servings

1. Have your child combine all ingredients in medium microwavable bowl, stirring to coat evenly.
2. Microwave on high for 3 minutes, and stir.
3. Transfer hot cereal into individual serving bowls and serve.

. . . . . . . . . . . . . . . .

Note: Young children should be supervised when handling hot foods.

. . . . . . . . . . . . . . . .

# Turkey Club Buns

*Easy-to-assemble lunches are perfect for lazy weekends, and this club sandwich is a winner.*

4 whole wheat burger buns
2 tablespoons reduced-fat
   mayonnaise
2 tablespoons ready-made
   bacon bits
4 slices turkey breast
   lunchmeat
4 slices 2%-fat American
   cheese
4 thin slices tomato

Estimated preparation time: 5 minutes
Makes 4 sandwiches

1. Have your child open the burger buns, spread each side with dab of the mayonnaise, and sprinkle with bacon bits.
2. Ask your child to layer (on each bun bottom round) turkey, cheese, and tomato slices, place bun tops on the sandwiches, and serve.

# Bologna Wrap Sandwiches

4 medium flour tortillas
2 tablespoons reduced-fat
    mayonnaise
4 large lettuce leaves
4 slices bologna
4 slices 2%-fat American
    cheese
4 thin slices tomato

*Kids love bologna, and burrito-type sandwiches break lunchtime monotony.*

Estimated preparation time: 5 minutes
Makes 4 sandwiches

1. Have your child spread each flour tortilla with a dab of mayonnaise, and layer with lettuce, bologna, cheese, and tomato slices.
2. Carefully fold sides of each tortilla to overlap on the center. Secure with toothpick and serve.

# Golden Tuna Bagels

*Bagels are another way to make a "boring" sand-wich better, and this tuna treat is nutritious as well.*

4 egg bagels, sliced in half
1 can (6 ounces) water-packed
    tuna, drained
4 slices 2%-fat American
    cheese
4 thin slices tomato

Estimated preparation time: 5 minutes
Estimated baking time: 5 minutes
Makes 4 sandwiches

1. Preheat oven to 350 degrees.
2. Help your child assemble each bagel sandwich by layer-ing tuna, cheese, and tomato slices on bottom round, and topping with upper round.
3. Place sandwiches on nonstick cookie sheet and bake for 5 minutes.

# Brawny Beef Sub

2 tablespoons reduced-fat mayonnaise
2 tablespoons fat-free Caesar salad dressing
1 loaf (8 ounces) French bread, cut in half lengthwise
½ pound thinly sliced deli roast beef
4 to 5 fresh spinach leaves
1 medium tomato, thinly sliced

*Older children will love preparing this colossal sandwich for the family.*

Estimated preparation time: 5 minutes
Makes 4 servings

1. Help your child mix together mayonnaise and Caesar dressing. Spread on each half of loaf.
2. Ask your child to assemble sliced beef, spinach leaves, and tomato on bottom half of loaf. Add top half of loaf, cut into 4 sections, and serve.

# Fruit and Tuna Salad Boats

*This eye-appealing entrée is as fun to make as it is to eat!*

Estimated preparation time: 10 minutes
Makes 4 servings

1. Have your child place tuna, pineapple, and raisins in medium bowl and stir to combine.
2. Add salad dressing and toss gently.
3. Allow your child to spoon mixture into each cantaloupe quarter.

1 can (6 ounces) water-packed tuna, drained
1 can (6 ounces) crushed pineapple, drained
1 cup raisins
½ cup raspberry vinaigrette dressing
1 medium cantaloupe, quartered and seeded

# Stuffed-Crust Pita Pizzas

6 whole wheat pitas
6 slices 2%-fat mozzarella
    cheese
$\frac{1}{3}$ cup tomato sauce
1 teaspoon Italian seasoning
3 slices turkey salami,
    chopped
1 cup reduced-fat shredded
    pizza blend cheese

*This recipe has been a huge success in my home, and your children will love preparing and eating it, too.*

Estimated preparation time: 10 minutes
Estimated baking time: 12 to 15 minutes
Makes 6 servings

1. Preheat oven to 375 degrees.
2. Help your child slice openings into the side of the pitas. Have your child slide 1 slice of mozzarella cheese into each pocket.
3. Place filled pitas on a nonstick cookie sheet. Spread 1 tablespoon tomato sauce evenly on top of each pita and sprinkle with Italian seasoning. Allow your child to arrange chopped salami on each pizza, then top with shredded cheese.
4. Bake for 12 to 15 minutes, remove, cool slightly, and serve.

Note: Be sure to keep young children away from the hot oven.

# Hot Diggity Dog Pie

*This surprising casserole is a tasty treat for the whole family.*

Estimated preparation time: 10 minutes
Estimated baking time: 20 minutes
Makes 6 servings

1. Preheat oven to 375 degrees.
2. Have your child place contents of cornbread mix in medium bowl, add water, and stir until well combined. Help your child fold in contents of canned chili sauce.
3. Lightly coat 10-inch pie pan with cooking oil spray. Have your child spoon in the cornbread mixture, and arrange franks in fan design on top of the batter.
4. Bake for 20 minutes, remove from oven, cool, and serve.

1 package (7.5 ounces)
    cornbread mix
½ cup water
1 can (10 ounces) hot dog
    chili sauce
cooking oil spray
6 beef or turkey franks

# Ravioli Casserole

cooking oil spray
2 packages (12 ounces each)
    fresh spinach ravioli
1 can (8 ounces) tomato sauce
1½ cups low-fat cottage
    cheese
1 can (15 ounces) Italian-style
    diced tomatoes
1 cup reduced-fat shredded
    mozzarella cheese

*My boys love ravioli, and this dish is very easy to prepare.*

Estimated preparation time: 10 minutes
Estimated baking time: 20 minutes
Makes 6 generous servings

1. Preheat oven to 375 degrees.
2. Lightly coat $9 \times 13$-inch baking dish with cooking oil spray. Have your child arrange ravioli from one package on the bottom of the dish.
3. Help your child make layers: Spread entire contents of tomato sauce over raviolis, followed by layer of cottage cheese. Arrange remaining raviolis on top of the cottage cheese layer. Spoon and spread entire contents of canned diced tomatoes over the second ravioli layer, and sprinkle with shredded cheese.
4. Cover baking dish with foil and bake for 20 minutes, until heated through.

# Earthquake Taco Salad

*Children of all ages love to shake up this terrific dinner.*

Estimated preparation time: 10 minutes
Makes 6 to 8 servings

1. Have your child place the chicken, beans, tomato, olives, and salad greens in 1-gallon plastic bag. Seal tightly and shake vigorously.
2. Help your child transfer mixture to large salad bowl.
3. Sprinkle with shredded cheddar cheese and serve with dressings of your choice or over a bed of tortilla chips.

2 cups diced, cooked chicken meat
1 can (16 ounces) kidney beans, rinsed and drained
1 medium tomato, diced
1 can (2.25 ounces) sliced black olives, drained
1 package (16 ounces) salad greens
½ cup reduced-fat shredded cheddar cheese
salad dressing
1 bag (16 ounces) tortilla chips (optional)

# Bread Bowl Chicken Taco Salad

1 round loaf of bread
    (8 ounces), with the
    center cut out to form
    bowl
3 to 4 large lettuce leaves
2 cups diced cooked chicken
    meat
½ cup mild salsa
½ cup reduced-fat shredded
    cheddar cheese

*Another tasty taco dinner, this time served in a bread bowl. This recipe works well on a night when you don't want to heat up the kitchen.*

Estimated preparation time: 5 minutes
Makes 4 servings

1. Have your child line bread bowl with lettuce leaves.
2. Have your child combine diced chicken and salsa in small bowl.
3. Spoon onto lettuce, sprinkle with shredded cheese, and serve.

# Frozen Yogurt Pops

*This cool and fruity dessert is so simple even a toddler can put it together.*

8 snack-size containers
(4 ounces each)
nonfat fruit yogurt
8 clean popsicle sticks

Estimated preparation time: 5 minutes
Estimated freezing time: 6 to 8 hours
Makes 8 yogurt pops

1. Help your child make small slits in the center of the wrapping on the top of each container.
2. Carefully slide popsicle sticks into slits and down into yogurt.
3. Freeze for 6 to 8 hours or overnight. Carefully remove frozen pops from containers before serving by rolling the sides between your palms for a moment to loosen them.

# Chewy Oatmeal Bars

1 can (6 ounces) frozen
    unsweetened apple
    juice concentrate,
    thawed
2 tablespoons unflavored
    gelatin (such as Knox
    brand)
4 cups old fashioned oats
½ cup raisins

*These chewy, low-fat, low-sugar bars are a healthy alternative to packaged treats.*

Estimated preparation time: 10 minutes
Estimated cooking time: 3 minutes
Estimated refrigeration time: 1 hour
Makes 16 servings

1. Have your child place apple juice concentrate in medium microwavable bowl.
2. Microwave on high for 3 minutes. Remove.
3. Add unflavored gelatin and stir until dissolved. Quickly add oats and raisins, tossing well to coat evenly.
4. Have your child spread mixture into $9 \times 9$-inch baking dish and refrigerate for 1 to 2 hours, or until set. Cut into 16 bars.

· · · · · · · · · · · · · · · ·

Note: Young children should be carefully supervised when handling hot liquids.

· · · · · · · · · · · · · · · ·

228          Culinary Kids

# Rainbow Melon Wedges

*Kids are crazy about this colorful, zany fruit dessert.*

Estimated preparation time: 15 minutes
Estimated cooking time: 8 to 10 minutes
Estimated refrigeration time: 15 to 30 minutes
Makes 8 to 12 servings

1 cup unsweetened
    applesauce
1 package strawberry flavored
    gelatin (4-serving size)
1 cup nonfat plain yogurt
1 cup fresh blueberries
2 medium melons, halved,
    seeded, and patted dry

1. Help your child pour applesauce into a small saucepan and bring to boil over medium heat. Stir in gelatin until dissolved.
2. Refrigerate until quite thick but not set, about 15 minutes.
3. Have your child stir in yogurt, and beat at highest speed until doubled in volume. Stir in blueberries.
4. Have your child spoon whipped mixture into melon halves and chill until firm. Cut each half to serve.

. . . . . . . . . . . . . . . .

Note: Small children should be kept away from a hot stove, although older children can prepare this with adult supervision.

. . . . . . . . . . . . . . . .

# Red, White, and Blue Graham Towers

1 package (8 ounces) reduced-
   fat cream cheese,
   softened
¼ cup sugar
½ teaspoon grated lime peel
½ teaspoon almond extract
1 pint strawberries, sliced
2 pints blueberries
24 graham cracker squares

*Simple and patriotic, these healthy treats make great snacks, too. The creamed mixture holds most of the fruit in place, but like S'mores, the mess is half the fun of eating these.*

Estimated preparation time: 10 minutes
Makes 8 servings

1. Have your child combine cream cheese, sugar, lime peel, and almond extract in medium bowl, and stir until smooth. Gently stir in ½ cup strawberries and ½ cup blueberries.
2. Spread each of 16 graham squares with 1 tablespoon cream cheese mixture. Sprinkle with about ⅔ remaining strawberries and blueberries.
3. To assemble, place one cheese-covered graham square on top of second, then top with plain graham square. Garnish with remaining fruit.

# Pecan Cookies

*The next time your children ask to bake cookies, try this streamlined "homemade" recipe.*

Estimated preparation time: 15 minutes
Estimated baking time: 8 to 12 minutes
Makes 4 dozen cookies

1 package (1 pound 10 ounce)
    chocolate chip cookie
    mix
1 egg
1 tablespoon water
$\frac{1}{3}$ cup unsweetened
    applesauce
2 cups pecan halves

1. Preheat oven to 375 degrees.
2. Have your child place cookie mix into large bowl. Stir in egg, water, and applesauce until thoroughly moist, taking care to break up any large lumps.
3. Drop rounded teaspoonsful of dough onto lightly greased cookie sheet. Place pecan half in the center of each cookie.
4. Bake for 8 to 9 minutes for chewy cookies, 10 to 12 minutes for crisper cookies. Remove from oven and allow to cool for 1 minute, then remove to cooling rack.

# Index

**236** Index

Index      **237**

# International Conversion Chart

These are not exact equivalents: they've been slightly rounded to make measuring easier.

LIQUID MEASUREMENTS

| American | Imperial | Metric | Australian |
|---|---|---|---|
| 2 tablespoons (1 oz.) | 1 fl. oz. | 30 ml | 1 tablespoon |
| ¼ cup (2 oz.) | 2 fl. oz. | 60 ml | 2 tablespoons |
| ⅓ cup (3 oz.) | 3 fl. oz. | 80 ml | ¼ cup |
| ½ cup (4 oz.) | 4 fl. oz. | 125 ml | ⅓ cup |
| ⅔ cup (5 oz.) | 5 fl. oz. | 165 ml | ½ cup |
| ¾ cup (6 oz.) | 6 fl. oz. | 185 ml | ⅔ cup |
| 1 cup (8 oz.) | 8 fl. oz. | 250 ml | ¾ cup |

SPOON MEASUREMENTS

| American | Metric |
|---|---|
| ¼ teaspoon | 1 ml |
| ½ teaspoon | 2 ml |
| 1 teaspoon | 5 ml |
| 1 tablepoon | 15 ml |

OVEN TEMPERATURES

| Fahrenheit | Centigrade | Gas |
|---|---|---|
| 250 | 120 | ½ |
| 300 | 150 | 2 |
| 325 | 160 | 3 |
| 350 | 180 | 4 |
| 375 | 190 | 5 |
| 400 | 200 | 6 |
| 450 | 230 | 8 |

WEIGHTS

| US/UK | Metric |
|---|---|
| 1 oz. | 30 grams (g) |
| 2 oz. | 60 g |
| 4 oz. (¼ lb) | 125 g |
| 5 oz. (⅓ lb) | 155 g |
| 6 oz. | 185 g |
| 7 oz. | 220 g |
| 8 oz. (½ lb) | 250 g |
| 10 oz. | 315 g |
| 12 oz. (¾ lb) | 375 g |
| 14 oz. | 440 g |
| 16 oz. (1 lb) | 500 g |
| 2 lbs. | 1 kg |